THE CREED OF CHRIST

The
CREED OF CHRIST

An Interpretation of the Lord's Prayer

GERALD HEARD

Eugene, Oregon

Wipf and Stock Publishers
199 W 8th Ave, Suite 3
Eugene, OR 97401
www.wipfandstock.com

The Creed of Christ
An Interpretation of the Lord's Prayer
By Gerald Heard
Copyright © 1940 Gerald Heard
Copyright renewed 1968 by Gerald Heard
Copyright transferred to The Barrie Family Trust
Foreword/Synopsis: Copyright © 2007 by John Roger Barrie

ISBN 13: 978-1-55635-097-9
ISBN 10: 1-55635-097-X

Publication date: 1/1/2008
Previously published by Harpers & Brothers, 1940

Photograph of Gerald Heard by Jay Michael Barrie

To

ALLAN AND ELIZABETH HUNTER
this joint effort toward working out a Way

Series Foreword

Gerald Heard (Oct. 6, 1889–Aug. 14, 1971) wrote nearly forty books during the course of a distinguished career. His Cambridge-trained, curiosity-ridden mind left no stone unturned in its intellectual investigations. His nonfiction topics ranged from history to philosophy, from psychology to religion, and virtually everything in between. These issues were woven together by a single unifying theme—the evolution of consciousness. During the 1940s, after he had relocated to America, after he had rediscovered his religious roots, and after he had begun a rigorous daily meditation practice, Gerald, as he was always known, mobilized his energies into establishing Trabuco College in Southern California. Trabuco was the first coeducational spiritual community in America to incorporate ecumenical, nonsectarian religious principles and practices. And practice the Trabuco attendees did, meditating three times daily in order to accelerate the spiritual evolution of their own individual consciousnesses.

Having previously published a dozen mostly academic and popular science books, Gerald turned his attention to religion during this war-torn decade. Gerald's religious writings from this period consist of eight key contributions that address practical and inspirational spiritual themes. Of these, four primary Heardian religious works are initially included in this vital new Wipf & Stock series, with more to follow. Collectively these books comprise Gerald's quintessential statements on the spiritual path, and a person could conceivably use these volumes as guidebooks for their entire spiritual journey.

And here is Gerald at his very best—preaching the evolution of consciousness and offering practical advice on how to attain it. Gerald's rotating roles as visionary historian, maverick cosmologist, and prescient philosopher are all present in the background of these religious works. But at the forefront is Gerald the practicing mystic and knowing docent, gushing forth an ebullient but sometimes cautionary narrative on traversing the spiritual path from start to finish. His accounts, as confirmed by classic mystics and traditional texts, derive from his own subjective experience. The ringing truth of his musings will cause the receptive reader first to reflect, then to act, propelled by the stirring contagion of Gerald's boundless enthusiasm.

In the 1940s, novelist Christopher Isherwood wrote that Gerald, "has influenced the thought of our time, directly and indirectly, to an extent which will hardly be appreciated for another fifty years." Those fifty years have now passed. Some of Gerald's ideas have fallen by the wayside, while others lie dormant still waiting to sprout. Yet a good many have blossomed into unspoken cornerstones of contemporary thought. The widespread establishment of religious communities has become commonplace. Religious syncretism, ecumenical studies, and interdisciplinary, eclectic approaches lie at the vanguard of progressive religious

Series Foreword

thought. Contemplative meditation practices have gained broad acceptance across a spectrum of diverse traditions. Theories on the evolution of consciousness abound. Colleges and whole movements of thought now regularly explore the transpersonal realm of pure consciousness.

But what makes Gerald's farsighted approach to religion especially relevant now is what made it relevant when these books were first published—he is espousing timeless truths. The reader is supplied with a map, compass, and numerous exhortations of attainment, as well as warnings of the pitfalls to avoid while embarking on this singlemost important sojourn in life. Gerald offered no quick fixes or shortcuts. He advocated a wholesale restructuring of one's entire being through, "the skilled, conscious training of our spirits." He advanced a holistic approach long before holistic approaches became popular.

Within these books is found Gerald's essential message: "Our whole life must become intentional and purposive, instead of a series of irrelevant events, adventures, and accidents. We must ourselves deliberately develop ourselves. That evolution which follows will show itself in a threefold development: in growth of conduct, of character and of consciousness itself. The world exists for man to achieve union with God. The meaning of all, the purpose and the end of all is one thing, seeing God."

When revisiting Gerald's spiritual classics in this new century, we are entering the very heart of religious experience. We are treading the path trodden by serious spiritual practitioners, be they novices or seasoned

Series Foreword

mystics. We are undertaking a journey of utmost significance, leading to pulsating union with God. As able guide and modern interpreter of mysticism, Gerald Heard nimbly and authoritatively beckons us toward the Goal that each of us was born to realize in this very life.

John Roger Barrie
Literary Executor of Gerald Heard
Nevada City, California
January 22, 2007

Thanks especially to Ted Lewis of Wipf and Stock Publishers, and Craig Tenney and Phyllis Westberg of Harold Ober Associates for their valuable assistance in bringing this series into print.

For more information on Gerald Heard, visit geraldheard.com, the Gerald Heard Official Website.

—JRB

CONTENTS

I. INTRODUCTION.	The Signature Prayer	1
II. THE NOTATION.	"Hallowed be Thy Name"	34
III. THE KINGDOM.	"Thy Kingdom come; on Earth as in Heaven"	63
IV. THE BREAD.	"Give us this day the Bread of the Coming Day"	85
V. THE FORGIVENESS.	"Forgive us our debts as we forgive"	110
VI. THE END OF EVIL.	"Deliver us from The Evil"	141

THE CREED OF CHRIST

I. INTRODUCTION

The Signature Prayer

❖❖❖❖❖❖❖❖❖❖❖❖❖❖❖❖❖❖❖❖❖❖❖❖❖❖❖❖❖❖❖❖❖

When that dominant liberal statesman of Britain, William Ewart Gladstone, died, there was a dispute over the memorial. Now that the master-voice was stilled, how best might his leadership be remembered, his initiative be organized? There was no doubt that he had crystallized liberalism into a political force of the first magnitude. He found a number of ideas of humanistic good will and a number of intelligent politicians without prestige or a policy. He left a party which led the country and recruited almost all political talent because it could find expression and place for all progressive and practical intelligence. Memorials are traditional: the weighty and obvious members of the party held for something conventional—a statue certainly, a hall probably, some scholarships perhaps. But as the party itself was new and progressive, a few of the still newer men advocated a departure. Liberalism, they said, cannot rest on its laurels. The future will not lie with it unless, as true progressives, the party members make that future. The people must know the party, not merely as standing for a policy or even a philosophy, but also as a succinct faith, a faith-in-a-phrase, a slogan.

"Put some of the memorial fund," they therefore said, "into a prize for the best rally song. Liberalism must have its Signature Tune." They were defeated. Such a fancy was too psychological for practical men. Today in Britain liberalism has been dead for twenty years. Yet such advice might have been heeded. "He who makes a nation's songs. . . ." is old and well-proved counsel.

For indeed this necessity for a group-rallying exercise is not new. Movements older than political bodies have had and have had to have their corporate affirmations. Churches have always needed to face this problem—how best to preserve, convey, and carry on the essence of their Founder's teaching when he is gone. And the same division of opinion has always shown itself. Some have felt that a monument was and must be the right nucleation point: the Holy Places, the Cave of the Nativity and that of the Sepulchre; the Holy Relics, the True Cross, the Nails, the Seamless Robe. Others were certain that a codified definition was best—a credal condensation of the Founder's philosophy. A third party was convinced that a biography was the one safe anchor. From a collection of approved "lives" the Church could best learn how to work out the sequel.

As a historical fact the real issue came to lie between the narratives and the definitions, between the collected books of biography and comment and the creeds. Loyalty was made to depend pre-eminently on one or the other of these two. The creeds certainly appeared for some considerable time to be the winning way. They were terse and definite. The biographies, as narratives must, told a story; they did not rally a party. As time has gone on, however, the creeds have tended more to separate than to unite. It has become clear that they attempted to condense too much and to define too far. Religion is concerned with life, with a process. Beyond a point, definition becomes limitation. In order to act we need to make certain hypotheses about the universe, but all action will become arrested, all actual advance be frustrated (largely through our energy going in disputes), if the hypotheses, instead of being used as means to gain more knowledge, are accepted as final dogmas to be enforced. About the Final Things, about the ultimate nature of Reality, we can at present know very little. In fact we can know only enough to know our ignorance and how, by recognizing it, to set about lessening it. Religion exists not to tell us, as we are, what Reality is. We could not understand that in our present condition. It is to show us the means whereby we may reach that end and become beings who can grasp such utter knowledge. The failure of creeds seems then to be that they attempted to handle as ends and entities certain facts which at our present state we can only deal with as means, as functions. Hence, while men have disputed about what they strove to define but could not produce, their disputing, which itself could never bring them either knowledge or agreement, prevented them from undertaking that action, that training, that following-out of instruction in spiritual living and evolution which would have brought them to true understanding and union.

The discrediting of the creeds did not, however, leave those who depended on the biographies (the men of the Book in contrast to the men of the Church) able to give a new lead in religion. The difficulty of basing one's life on a biography became increasingly severe as the biographical material was examined. Contingent facts of history, it was now maintained, could never establish eternal values of the soul. The temporal conditions of a specific time, date, environment, and culture rendered it almost impossible to apply as universal rulings the actions and words of a teacher situated in, influenced by, and involved with peculiar local issues. Yet if the teaching did not apply everywhere and always, what precisely was its value, how much credit and what degree of modification must it have? It became necessary, therefore, to search in the biographies for something nodal, to disengage the essence from the accretions and interpretations of the reporters obsessed with their immediate problem, to find the element of universality, to extract in enduring propositions the way of life which had been not only taught but lived.

Does not this, however, lead us straight back to where we started? Are not the creeds precisely this thing, the first of such efforts at essence-extraction, such isolation of the active, life-giving, eternal element out of the temporal and the accidental? And are not the Higher Criticisms the end of such efforts —the germ itself reduced to inert chemicals? Nevertheless, a third possibility does exist; hope lies at the end of another approach. If the teaching in the biographies was not intended to give a complete cosmology, if the very simplicity of the theology is intentional, not because the teacher was uninformed, but because those to be taught were and are incapable of more understanding until by obeying them have grown, then we must not look for a closed, complete system; we must see if we can discover advices for a way of life.

That, of course, has been a not unfamiliar recommendation. But if true, why has it not produced more remarkable results? Once again, even here it seems that this advice started too far ahead for most of us. Leaving aside theology, not because it was necessarily untrue in itself, but because we may still be at such a level as to be unable either to judge it or to use it, the constructive critics rightly wished to start with the actual teaching. That, they found, coagulated in those pristine passages which seemed, textually, closest to actual notes taken by listeners and morally loftiest. But when considered as advice for every immediate action, the Sermon on the Mount with its core of Beatitudes presented great difficulties. Soon it, too, was in pieces—dissections and amputations, caused not so much by the textual difficulty of deciding whether the words were ever spoken as by the moral difficulty of resolving whether they could ever be practiced. It is there, undoubtedly, that the difficulty lies and it is of supreme gravity. We are familiar with the objections: "Oriental hyperbole," "a villager's false simplification of civilization's issues," "the ethic for an Interim" (sitting it out in a spiritual Zoar while God blasts Sodom into submission), "the enthusiastic optimism of a Nature poet." These explanations must be faced. The Sermon on the Mount tells us what to do, what will happen if we do it, and what must happen if we don't. But it does not tell us how to do it. It is true that though it may be the only morality which does not end by denying itself, it will not work of itself, like a law of nature. It has to work in and through us. It therefore will never work unless there is a method whereby we may learn to work it. Just to find it admirable, ideal, gets us nowhere. Indeed, we see what has happened to that very word "ideal." Meaning originally the utterly real behind all appearances, it has sunk until it simply stands for what we wish (or wish we could wish) but know to be impossible.

At the heart of the Gospels there is, however, one other thing. Beside the new Commandments, beside the new Law, more lovely but far more exacting than the old, there is, put even more briefly and tersely, a master-instruction, a set of key-rules as to how that Law may be kept. There is only one passage in the biographies more central than the Sermon on the Mount. It is more central because it is the root from which the action ordered by the Sermon must spring, because it shows the source of power without which the Sermon, the Beatitudes, remain a magnificent but impossible demand, a splendid promise which cannot be fulfilled. That passage is therefore rightly called by a supreme title, the Lord's Prayer. Christ was neither a dreamer building sky castles with poetic language nor a tyrant demanding bricks without straw. He told his disciples both what he had learned of his Father's laws and also how he had been taught to live them abundantly. He made no mystery of his power. He pointed to his works, told men to believe in them, as practical proof, if his teaching and being seemed beyond their grasp, told his followers that works such as his they should do. He told them that he gave because he had first received. He never suggested that he or anyone else could fulfill the divine will unless he was filled with the divine power. All his years of preparation did not make him feel that therefore he could, during the brief and pressing thirty-six months of his ministry, dispense with prayer. The decisive conviction of sonship at the Baptism; the decisive victory in the threefold initial ordeal of the Temptation; the clear recognition of his path, his goal, his relationship with his Father; his endowment with intense spiritual power; all these events and their consequences did not render him any less persistent in that constant recharging of his whole person through regular and profound communion with the spirit of his Father. He never seems to have thought that because his "meat" was "to do the will of Him who sent me," because of his devotion, dedication, and incessant service in that cause, because he was always helping, teaching, and salvaging others, therefore he was excused turning back to the source of all his grace and replacing patiently and carefully the virtue he spent so divinely. Because time was short and evil urgent, defiant, advancing, that, to him, did not mean that he must take not a moment off from helping the stricken and opposing the devil. "The best prayer is a good deed" would, if we are to judge by his acts, have seemed to him dangerously woolly and unreal thinking, the conclusion of one who really knew very little about real prayer, real good, or for that matter real evil and the only sort of power which real evil respects. We may judge by the ration of his life, the balance of his time, the way in which he allotted his days, the whole strategy of his campaign to rescue beleaguered man that even he, patiently prepared and incomparably endowed, considered any disregard of, any restriction on, the life of prayer to be a criminal mistake deserving the ruin of the entire enterprise. "Watch and pray that ye enter not into temptation, the spirit truly is willing but the flesh is weak"—perhaps one of his latest admonitions to his disciples—though it takes for granted a sincere wish, which is more than many can claim, still concludes that the sheer downswing of the body and the reflexes is sufficient to ruin a man unless he can order his life into a series of watches so that vigilance shall be practically unbroken and unsleeping.

If anyone might have been supposed to be able to keep in incessant, effortless, ample communion with his Father, whatever he was doing, wherever he was, surely it was he. Yet, as a matter of record we see that he never acted on that assumption—

that, because he was so busy and so effective in doing good, in teaching wisdom, in transmitting love, this was enough. He did often cease from doing, though often he took the time out of the hours we give to sleep, to give himself up wholly to receiving from the source and center of the divine wisdom, goodness, and love. His working life pivoted on prayer though he knew he was God's son. His ministry was an alternation between absorption in God and transmission to man. The latter was never a substitute for the former but evidently remained continuously dependent on the former. Indeed, it seems to be conveyed in the biographies that this was so, was necessarily so, because by this alternation, by these spells of utter communion he was, even throughout the three brief years of ministry, still growing in further powers; the radiation which he transmitted was, to the close, gaining in volume, if not in purity of transmission.

Each stage of his life was initiated by a climax of communion—in the desert before his Temptation; before freeing the boy maniac from the intense possession; before the resolve to go up to Jerusalem and die. Indeed, it seems from these accounts necessary to conclude, as did the writer of the letter to the Hebrews when explaining this life, that here was no Demiurge—a godlike being free of human limitations, who like some spiritual insect was suddenly, at Baptism, precipitated, hatched, into a completed, undeveloping perfection, as a master-teacher stocked with verbally inspired sermons and infallible repartees, an equipment of demonstrative miracles and a fixed program of salvation. On the contrary here was one who because he was supremely man, the "firstfruits" of a fully human ascent to God, lived a life to the end outstandingly marked by the one supreme human characteristic: youthfulness; or we may use his own word, the word today rediscovered, on their own, by the evolutionists: childfulness.

It is this inherent power to prevent growing up from meaning—as it does mean with all other animals save man—hardening up, closing in; it is this power of being full formed in stature and yet supple, free, and open in spirit, which is man's unique endowment and on which his supremacy depends. Far longer than any other animal man remains a child, so much a child that he is called "the foetalization of the ape," and by that refusal to set and harden, to close his mind and toughen his heart, he enters on a station of life, a state of being, which puts all the other animals below him and in his power, for "his thoughts are not their thoughts nor his ways their ways, he is above their mind and their heart." But though he is still innocent, un-guarded, un-"knowing" when the kitten's play has turned into the cat's stupid cruelty and even when the young ape's fun and curiosity have cockled into suspicion and cunning, man himself fails to go on to the full range of his promise. He fails to live more than one-seventh of his whole life in his first innocency. He cannot sustain the promise of his early years. That first trust, and wonder and realization of his own ignorance, and direct poignancy at beauty and suffering—all that clearness of vision, that single-heartedness, clouds over and corrodes. He fails to remain a child, to retain, with every fresh extension of power and perspective, the original supreme gift of being interested by everything and finding everyone appealing. But he who saw, and knew why the Kingdom of his Father could alone be entered by becoming like a child, he himself so lived. He was the Son of Man, because, though greater than any of his generation, he was their junior, he was younger, he belonged, by the creative power which he allowed to keep flowing in renewal through him, to a generation of men who, even now after two thousand years, have yet to be born. Continually by that daily rejuvenation and renewal of humility, trust, and wonder he cast off the creeping shroud of complacency, indifference, and concession to things as men maintain they must be. So he continually achieved new powers, continually opened out into new capacities and fulfillments, continually brought out from the stored treasure deposited with him by his Father. He never ceased releasing these inherent riches because he kept them solvent by exposing his entire nature to the liquidating radiation of his Father's presence. Hence to the end he will yield new characteristics, new essentials of being, until he, the archetypal man, can say, must say, "I and my Father are One," for man may be, must be, all that God may be in Time.

One is aware that so to estimate this figure is to

be charged by students of historical documents with a wish to make a man into a Demiurge. This, however, is a question not of the Lower Criticism, or textual judgment and estimate, but of the Higher Criticism, of what seems to one to be probable and possible. Here everyone has a right to bring such knowledge as he has formed of man during the time he has been a human being and lived among mankind. "What think ye of Christ?" The question has never ceased or been settled from the first day of his ministry until this moment. The answers depend mainly on what we know of man's nature. When the possible developments of the primates were unknown, people mocked at the stories, from Hanno to Du Chaillu, of a manlike creature but huge as three men, who could pluck a man's arm out of its socket as we pluck a radish from the earth and bend iron as a strong man bends a sapling. Yet the gorilla has proved to have all these inhuman physical powers and more. If we have never had the opportunity, never gone on the search, to explore saintliness; if, on the contrary, we have kept to our studies and thought of scholarship as the height of human development, we can have no notion to what extremes holiness may rise. Whatever the Christ of the Gospels may be, he is not presented to us as a scholar or even as "a man of the mean," a gentleman whose motto is Tallyrand's instruction for the diplomat, *"pas de zèle."* We are told that those who saw him had quite the contrary impression, for they "remembered it was written, The zeal of thy house has eaten me up."

There is undoubtedly more than a suggestion of a white heat of being, of an intensity of consciousness, far closer to the incandescent focus of creative genius, the integral thought and action of the supreme artist, the inspired creator, than to the cool, critical, analytical intelligence of the collector. Studies of sainthood are, however, now being made and after scores of sham reputations have been reduced to meretricious dust in the critic's crucible, a number of lives resist any further analysis; they remain inexplicably anomalous. For accounts of some such we do not have to go back far; we can see them as it were in the round, viewed from several angles by different observers. Such men do for human history and for the upper level of man's development what the discovery of the gorilla has done for natural history and for the aberrant range of primate evolution. We realize that we far too lightly assumed that what we saw close about us was the utmost range of life's capacity. These outgrowths are rare but they have hardly ceased to be recorded for every generation of mankind.

That is the first point; sainthood does exist and, quite apart from its goodness, it is a quality of being, a range of consciousness of such intensity, such singleness of spirit, that it may well be estimated as being another species of human creature, as far as character is concerned. The second point is that such men, quite apart from their other uses, are the only ones adequate to pass an opinion on their own species, its nature and powers, and further species, above even themselves, should such superbeings exist. It is a fact of historical importance that many of the authentic saints have repeatedly asserted, and indeed maintained as though it were an obvious fact, that Christ was far higher above them than they are above us. That judgment we cannot dismiss out of hand. If I have never seen a Velásquez but only rather confused photographs, while an artist, whose power to paint striking likenesses is utterly beyond my skill, tells me that there is a greater gap between his art and that of the master than between my scrawls and his own competent portraits, I may not be able to see that this is so; I should, however, be wise to bow to the judgment. That, putting it crudely, as must all illustrations of the greater by the less, is much our position in regard to the Founder of Christianity. The critics have too often stepped in and ruled what such a being could do by the laws of probability which have formed in their minds while they have lived lives which were both restricted in experience and of quite modest, if respectable, moral and spiritual attainment. They lived in the clear, and weak, radiation which is characteristic of the center of the human spectrum. Of the appalling pain-giving power of the infra-red, in its form of heat; still less of the utterly strange forces of the ultra-violet; of real evil and real good they never knew. We can then say that both what the saints have shown themselves to be—their very strange psychophysical behavior, their endurance, and their powers—and what they have maintained about the figure of Christ make it far harder to put that figure into an easy and familiar category. What if, after all, he is the Son of Man, a being belonging to an order to which up to the present hardly a single human being, perhaps none, has as yet belonged? How can we then judge him and say offhand what are his powers and what his nature? If he is at least one who was so essentially human that he continued developing long beyond that limit at which the best of us reach the lintel of a mental age which all the rest of our years will never permit us to raise by a month, then we should expect him to continue to grow in powers; and even the Fourth Gospel would be psychologically accurate when it makes the raising of Lazarus the climax of the human career.

A new question arises here: If Christ was a new birth, a new species; if man's task is to be so reborn as to become of that species; if, as we shall see in later chapters, this rebirth among those who have begun it is at least a double process of death and then rebirth, and the death is a terrible crisis of despair and apparent abandonment; did Christ, who retained this constant touch with his Father, follow in this respect the path which those who have followed him find? The answer seems to be both yes and no. The struggle is, we see, to keep in touch with Eternal Life; to keep accepting and never denying when the rest have sunk to a "knowing" denial; to keep on understanding when the rest have decided that the whole has no meaning; to keep on loving when the rest have resigned themselves to exclusion, "righteous anger," "necessary" hate. The higher the man, the more sensitive he is, the more he will be aware of the necessity of so keeping in touch with life, with love, with light —with his Father. He therefore will avoid one of our despairs. Aware every moment of his essential contact with eternity, he will be able instantly to sense anything which is beginning to cut off or screen out that radiation and so he will always be moving into the Light, however thickly the clouds are appearing in the sky. With our dull spiritual apprehension the sky is completely overcast and the life in us is already gravely chilled before we notice and remedy, at cost, our lack of vital vigilance; we have drifted far off our course, so careless are we in watching our compass and have to be involved in shoals and storms before we wake to the fact that we have lost our way. Hence we have many wasteful and dangerous spells spent in fighting our way back against the gale.

Such sloth and dullness does not afflict the Sons. Yet it seems they too have their crises, their deaths before each new rising to still-newer Life. Such seems to have been the Temptation; such perhaps the ordeal, lightly noted by the biographers, which culminates in the Transfiguration and the resolve to die. We may ask, was not the resolve, so to accept what seemed the Father's dark will the reason and cause of the Illumination? The depth of the fore-running darkness may perhaps be faintly gauged by the denunciation of Peter, the man he trusted as the only one who had recognized his true nature, as the devil, because Peter suggests an easier course.

The penumbra shadow of that returning darkness may account for the tensions of the last Temple scenes culminating in the sudden stroke at the sacerdotal business traffic. And such a deathly darkness, such a totality of eclipse, is signaled in the cry of utter desolation from the cross. If this is so, then the cross takes on a still further significance, for on it the Son of Man was actually born to a still-higher station and rank of being. If this is so, then we see also how the resurrection is integral to the death. The death on the cross was not merely physical; it was, on this showing, spiritual also. Jesus of Nazareth had gone as far as a Son of Man may go, in the vehicle and limitations of a man among men. He died, not merely to give us an example, nor to accept willing his responsibility for us all and for the mistake of all temporal life; he died also for himself, that he might be reborn in the full power of the timeless life. This may be what those early earnest thinkers meant when one of them said, "He was perfected by his sufferings" and by his death, and the other insisted "Flesh and Blood cannot inherit the Kingdom of God." Spirituality at a certain height may have to transcend the limitations of our ordinary living. Perhaps only then did the Son of Man really accept the full "naughting" required for his timeless union with his Father; perhaps only then did the last traces of the treacherous hopes of messiahship and physical utopianism die. When, after the cry of desolation, came the "It is finished," closing the earthly ministry, perhaps then and then only ceased the last illusions about time, and with that dawned at once the full intensity of eternity. The final crisis of rebirth, the final holding on to the Eternal Life and casting off the husk of the temporal—a process followed for forty years—culminated with the triumphant crisis of physical death in the complete acceptance of Reality. So, as he commended his spirit to his Father's hands, at that moment he was already raised to the power of endless living.

Anyone who dares to try and think for himself on so grave and vital an issue and who ventures to share his attempt with others must strive to avoid vagueness or any statement which may read as disingenuously ambiguous. It seems unmistakable, to one acutely interested layman, that the textual evidence for the Resurrection is not legally binding—it could not be sustained in a court of law. If we stick to the documents, submitting them as our whole case and bringing forward nothing more, then the only conclusion seems to be one which brings no comfort either to the orthodox or to the inconoclast. It seems impossible to avoid the conclusion that something unforeseen, inexplicable, and having immediately the most striking results, did occur. It seems also equally impossible not to conclude that we shall never in any detail be sure, from the state and quality of the documents, what did take place. So, again, as in judging the whole of this strangest of histories, we are forced back to Higher Criticism—to our anthropological knowledge, our answers to the question what is man and what is his nature? But that phrase

Higher Criticism—it, too, may be misleading. It is becoming clear that we today can no longer be content with two courts of historical judgment. There are now, in point of fact, three criticisms, three levels and ranges of judgment, each to be heard in its turn, three courts of reference. There is the primary, basic, Low Criticism which one finds on the documents themselves. The actual documents (e.g., by papyrology) may be set at the following chronological and geographical limits: fairly near the events described; near enough, it may well be, for such events to be accepted as true, provided they do not offend against other canons ruling acceptance. So the Low Criticism hands the documents up to the next court, which should be called the Middle Criticism. This first establishes with the aid of all obtainable parallel and adjacent knowledge what was the normal, ordinary run of events, opinions, and ideas at the time when the documents were written and the events which the documents narrate took place. The contemporary religions, hopes, and traditions; the philosophies, prejudices, and phraseology are ranged with the political, economic, and social systems of the day. So a reconstructed environment is made. Scaled on this, the accounts given in the texts are arranged and so it is decided what parts may be given credence, what parts cannot be accepted as factual in our contemporary sense.

This is a wise way of establishing the authenticity of normal historical events. It makes two assumptions, which may be safely made if the events being studied are normal. The first is that human nature does not alter and, moreover, never has a very wide range. Anyone may estimate the probable limits of any human character and capacity. We have already seen how this ruling may unconsciously bias experts long confined to restricted studies. The assumption also, of course, accepts the David Hume rejection of anomalous happenings on the ground that, as common sense knows the laws of nature and the limit of possible events, any report of an event which goes beyond our notion of common sense, however textually authenticated, must be rejected. Neither of these rulings stands clearly today. To take another example of the wide and exceptional range of human capacity: Who would not have said, before Mozart was born, that a musical prodigy of such power was beyond all probability and the descriptions of such a creature must be dismissed as obvious romancing? As to natural phenomena, exceptional happenings—there, too, man and his powers remain unknown. You cannot say what cannot happen. We now know that our knowledge depends not on strict causality but on probability, and our sense of probability mainly on what has happened to us and to people like us. Rarities are not impossibilities, though they may be nuisances to the orderly. Therefore the middle court cannot close the issue when it deals with the exceptional. So the Highest Criticism has to be summoned to sift these findings. The documents by themselves gain a verdict of "Non Proven"; it might have happened and it might not; it will depend on your other canons of criticism to which conclusion you will come. The knowledge of the time and place, of the environment and the mental climate—that set of judgments, too, yields a Non Proven. The central figure is certainly anomalous. If you happen to be of the opinion that such an unparalleled event could have taken place, because your world-view, your notion of cosmology, has place for such an irruption, well then, for you it is possible to believe. If, on the other hand, you feel that utter anomalies paralyze judgment, which of its nature must be based on comparison, then you will have to reject; you are debarred from believing.

But the third court has a further approach and makes a firmer contact. It owns that documents nearly two thousand years old are thin tissue in which to carry findings of such weight. It also agrees that a single, completely anomalous figure— one incomparable prodigy surrounded by nothing before, then, or since but ordinary men—is practically impossible to estimate. There is no scale, grade, or approach to forming any opinion about the historical likelihood of a theophany who stalks among men unaffected by them, uncomprehended by them, rootless in the earth around him, intruding from an inexplicable and alien order of being. But if we are able to be given in this third court findings of the Highest Criticism; if we are shown evidence of grades and approaches and scales of being; if we learn that there are orders of man, ranks and species of the human spirit, that there are Servants of God, then saints who are the Friends of God, and then above them the Sons; then we shall be able to glimpse an evolutionary order and ascent, a spiritual "phylum" or tree of life. Further, if we find that each step or grade has its own appropriate vision and power—as well as its rightful conduct—then, as we see the spiritual life as a complete evolutionary sequence, a continuance of the whole of evolution and following the laws of that progression, then we have at last, instead of inexplicable events (to which we have to reply, if we would not reject them, *credo quia impossibile*), a standard of true criticism. We have a critique by which to estimate the words, acts, conduct, and nature of one who calls himself the Son of Man and the Son of his Heavenly Father.

We cannot say what he can do, what is the upper limit of his powers and vision. But we are not compelled to reject events about him on the ground that, as such deeds and such events could neither be done nor be befallen by us, therefore they are impossible in relation to him. On the contrary, if we find ourselves compelled to estimate this man as one in many respects as much beyond and inexplicable to us as we are beyond and inexplicable to animals, then we see these facts as having their own inherent consistency and inner validity. A man, as man may be a million years ahead, should have, if evolution means anything, a different quality of consciousness, and so of behavior, acts, and psychophysical nature, than we now normally possess. Moreover, when we study "transitional types," men far above us but still far below this Man's record (to use the chronological language of evolution, men not a million years but half or only a quarter of a million years in advance), types, as we should expect, far commoner in occurrence and so able to be recorded far more frequently (and indeed, lately); when we find that such men already begin to show in rudiment, *in petto,* just those peculiar and startling departures from what we were taking to be the iron norm of man's nature; when we find that they are not merely intensely good but disconcertingly wise, insighted, and (indeed it must be owned, if we are to give a frank and full account) with powers of the mind-body which seem to us uncanny; then the evidence actually leads us to expect that the Son of Man would show the very characteristics, even the most startling ones, which the records maintain. He shows them naturally, inevitably; for they are the fruits of the evolutionary process, in which the lives of the good are the buds, the lives of the saints the flower. What would be unnatural would be if such a maturity came to no more than that embryonic degree of essential being and real power which we the good now express and command; if that full growth showed no fresh quality of nature but was simply a quantitative increase of what we now are.

A tree is diseased if all that happens as it grows is that its buds become no more than giant buds; that is not true growth but morbid hypertrophy. The trouble here does not lie in our lack of faith but in our blindness of vision. We are "fools and slow of heart": we realize that when the apple tree puts out its bud soon the bud will break open into flower and, in turn, the flower be cast in order that from its center a third completely new stage, the fruit, may take its place. We know, too, that only a child, tearing open the bud and finding no miniature flower within it, would deny that though there is no visible flower, still less fruit, in the bud while it is a bud, still the mysterious promise of its evolution *is* there and as the bud grows, so must be the flower and the fruit.

But in spite of that knowledge of life's way we fail to grasp the path of our own evolution; we are staggered and stumble at the thought that the same great rule of living nature rules us and makes at least equal promise to us—if we will pay the price. The whole principle of life is precisely in the fact which so startles us: Growth is not mechanical increase in size. We must not crudely "extrapolate." We do so because of two lacks: vision of what life might be and will to want so to live. It is all too easy to think we are growing because we are hypertrophying. That is our tragedy today, the tragedy of so much of our evil. It is the broad, easy path which looks as though it led to plenty, but leads in fact to destruction. True life does not follow the same line ad infinitum—that would be death, death on the dead-level, in a final congestion. The whole principle of evolution is a rising by steps, often by what seem striking, sudden, and indeed wildly dangerous and deadly steps from what appear to be the only sane levels of actuality to completely unsuspected manifestations of potentiality, to quite new ranges of being. In the Man of the Gospels we are then no longer faced with a sporadic outcrop, a single "sport," a being who may have lived but has never had the least cousinship with any of the sons of men; but, quite otherwise, we see a tremendous manifestation of a process and a promise which is always seeking to express itself in man and which has, time and again, if in different varieties and maybe with never yet such an intensity, still shown the promise of the Spirit. That, in brief, is the position to which one attempt to keep in touch with the witness of that Spirit, in East and West, in anthropology and theology, in hagiology and psychology, has brought a lay seeker.

So, viewing that life as one which, because of the fullness of the nature inspiring it, is a life of constant ascent up to its close, because it is never completed and ended as are ours—on the contrary, instead of reaching a limit and capacity of being, after which action takes the place of growth and, next, routine the place of action, that life goes on ever developing—we can see something further in the process of prayer which Christ followed to the end. The first evident reason for the extensive times given to prayer has been noted. It is one which we, even at our moderate level, can understand: exports must be balanced by imports —works can be accomplished only through power. Even the Sons of God while they work in the world know that, though the world is already and indeed always their Father's Kingdom, mankind is blinded to that fact and is behaving as though it were the devil's. Hence, against this black faith, so powerful in its blind conviction, even the Sons need constantly, consciously to seek their Father's presence, to stand back so as to look over the ocean of darkness at the over-spanning ocean of light.

The second reason for so great a place being given to prayer is deeper and outside the experience, or even the recognition, of all but the advanced. That is that prayer itself is not merely the preparation for action; it is action. And this is so not at all in the perfunctory sense in which we say *orare est laborare* (too often to be able to cancel out the first part with its complement, *laborare est orare*). Prayer of the highest quality—contemplation—is literally the creation of an atmosphere, an air in which the soul can begin to breathe, a radiation in which the spirit can mutate. Such intense activity brings the air of eternity into time, and our immortal nature, which is lying drugged and cataleptic within us, stirs and begins to come out of its coma. The holy, then, do not pray less as they become more holy. They pray more. Speech is a kind of surgery, necessary no doubt in certain cases but always doing some harm—however asepticized by humility and charity, doing some violence to the creature on whom it is used. Prayer is akin to radiation which heals the tumor without endangering the life of the patient. To argue with and convince a man of his evil is to run the risk of making him yield—if he does—not freely and to God but perforce and to superior dialectic or moral prestige. He may then become not a new creature, rising to union with God, but a slave, a creature who just wishes to be managed. It is these victories of dialectic and human moral ascendancy which have made the authoritarian churches worldly-wise, arrogantly intolerant, enforcing dogma with persecution.

Nor is this quality of prayer petitionary. Those who practice this life of communion-contemplation become perfectly open apertures through which pure, timeless Being radiates into time. Within the "field" which such natures precipitate, men find it natural to know that every soul is deathless and of infinite value. The spiritual climate becomes such in their presence that the crust of even the seeming dead begins to crack and show life underneath. Christ taught prayer because by that way of life he himself was never ceasing to become a further influence of extending power, because his radiation was becoming of always greater penetration, because he saw the evolution of his own life into the full knowledge of sonship and union as the first mutation of a new species of man, a new step, sheer and tremendous in the evolution of human consciousness.

Yet, once again it is necessary to note, there is no hastiness in spite of the urgency. Because the universe, he taught, exists that man, each individual, may come of his own free will to God, there can be no coercion, not even by spiritual power, still less by violence. Each must ask before he can receive. Liberation is a thing taken, not given. So, like all the greatest teachers, though he told men openly of the general destiny of man and pointed out their present pass and how they might deliver themselves, he gave the technical instruction only when his followers, having reflected on what he showed they must do, came to him asking how they were to find power to do it.

Such seems the place and significance of this prayer in the Gospels. And such seems to have been its history ever since. We are separated by creeds; we fall asunder when we assert and dispute over what we maintain that we have found and defined and what we hold others to have missed or misconstrued. We are united by prayer, we are brought together, when we own our ignorance, our helplessness, our uneradicated will to have our way, to dominate, and to exclude. The deeper the prayer, the more the self is lost in apprehension of the unspeakable One, the deeper is the unity, for unity with man is a by-product of union with the One and will only be accomplished in that way. For only in the intense focus of utter Being can the atomic hardness of our egos be fused. The mild warmth of good fellowship and mutual convenience leaves us fundamentally unchanged. We begin to grow, to transmute, and at last we actually recommend our faith when, instead of attempting to advocate, still less to enforce it (when we ourselves still remain such a grotesque parody of its claims), we set ourselves to be renatured by the skilled and developed process of prayer.

A priori, then, we might say that this prayer would be the seminal nucleus of a true religion. As a historical fact we know we have such a prayer at the very heart of Christianity. It is so brief, terse, condensed, that it is not difficult to hold these are the actual words spoken in answer to the simple man's inevitable demand for a group-unifying, self-transmuting method, for a means to live the Sermon on the Mount. It is so profound that it is even less difficult to accept that here we have the thought of a Son of God. In short, the more the prayer is studied, and the more it is compared with all the other means for defining and uniting Christian people, the more it seems clear that it is the one central and enduring postulate, the essential code, the real creed of Christianity.

That is why these brief, tentative addresses on the Lord's Prayer have been given the title "The Creed of Christ." The Lord's Prayer is the authentication, the signature, the demonstrating formula of all his teaching; it is the master-recipe for producing his demands, for reproducing his acts, for adopting not only his method but, if we will make this system our life, his nature. Here in epitome are the essential means and ends of his faith. Here is the practice, the exercise, whereby he was able to call himself the Son of Man, at last Man as God wills, and to call us through the same exercise and practice to rise to such sonship. By this prayer we may and must judge all Christianity, whether it is the millennial record of the Church or our own acts and thoughts of the last half-hour.

The five chapters which follow are reflections on the five main clauses. The substance of five addresses, given at the invitation of the Rev. Allan Hunter in his Mount Hollywood Congregational Church, these reflections are no more than the thoughts of a layman increasingly concerned with one urgent problem: Can human nature be changed? Can our real psychology, our practical science of human behavior be brought to a level where it may match our knowledge of physics? Can our power over ourselves be made as exact and extensive as our power over our outer environment? If we cannot do that, then it seems now obvious that because of this power over our environment we shall destroy ourselves. Academic psychology has, in this vital respect, failed us. Its science of the psyche has not given even the beginnings of such essential control. A professor of psychology is not immediately recognizable as one who has such powers even over himself. As a character, a creature of temperament, he is indistinguishable from a teacher of physics, a lawyer, or a politician. The practitioners of the most popular of applied psychologies, the psychoanalysts, by this practical test, reassure us no better.

In fact the only people who seem to be able to produce change in character are the religious. True, the numbers who so gain and grow in higher character control are small, but they are undeniable. Granted that this is a result of an applied process—that the growth of character is due to following a system (and not that characters capable

of adult-sustained growth always flock to religion)
—our chief and pressing need today is to discover
and elucidate that process. There would seem to
be at the heart of religion some method that does
alter character, can actually make super-characters,
and may, in rare but highly influential cases, actually create a new quality of consciousness. Here
then should lie, could it be stated in contemporary
terms, the answer to our moment's desperate challenge: to produce men adequate and able to sanction civilization, and a real psychology—a science
of spirit—adequate to balance our otherwise fatally
enlarged science of matter.

The hope which has grown while this masterprayer has been meditated on is briefly this: that
the mystics after all are right. They teach four
main things: Firstly, they say that Reality is not at
once apparent to us; we are blind and our blindness is difficult to cure because we see in our blind
eyes a false image and take this to be Reality.
Hence the source of all our troubles. Secondly, they
hold that Reality can be seen, if we will train to
recover our true sight. The single-hearted—those
who free their consciousness from the distortion of
greed and fear, from the illusion of the self—do
see God. Thirdly, as God is Reality, seeing Him is
not merely obtaining a right view of things as they
actually are; it is also a radiation, exposed to which
the spirit mutates. We become like what we see.
We see what the world is meant to be and we are
able to live as that world actually is in God's sight.
Fourthly, they teach that we are intended so to

evolve. The purpose of the world is not the establishment of a physical Utopia, though it is quite likely (it is certainly only so possible) that an economic paradise could be the by-product of a new humanity. The aim of creation is the evolution of life; that evolution, when it reaches human level, becomes the evolution of consciousness, and that evolution of consciousness rises through three stages; from servanthood, through friendship, to sonship.

The mystics are empiricists. Their theology and cosmology differ from that of the dogmatic theologians. They work from direct experience, are not concerned, as are the official ecclesiastical interpreters, to reconcile traditional authorities or to exclude innovations, but recognize that antinomies must be accepted. Because they are completely practical, only concerned with systems as means to a way of growth, their interest is not in terms and with the effort to define entities, but in processes and the elucidation functions. Theirs is the "algebraic" approach, in contradistinction to the "mathematical" approach of the theologian. Hence their basic postulate is that God is transcendent and immanent. His transcendence renders Him eminently immanent: His immanence is the clue to His transcendence. In definition, below this they will not yield; above this they will not talk. Here, they say, is a hypothesis, a strictly confined and working hypothesis, though it sounds paradoxical and extravagant. God is within you: enter and find Him, and you will find it is He who sustains and transcends space and time. Further words will only confuse you and delay you. Enter on the steep path. The way is sheer but open. The training is austere but rational. The means to climb are at hand. The view at the summit is Reality. Because you are now under illusion, you cannot, at this point, be told the nature of that view. Go and see. You can judge that it is not illusion by looking at those who have gone and seen. They were transformed by what they saw. So will you be.

The Lord's Prayer here is viewed as such a ladder to perfection.

II. THE NOTATION

"Hallowed be Thy Name."

✤✤✤✤✤✤✤✤✤✤✤✤✤✤✤✤✤✤✤✤✤✤✤✤✤✤✤✤✤✤✤✤✤✤✤✤✤✤

In the introductory chapter it became clear that the commonest objection people have to religion is that it seems to ask too much and help too little. It shows us the right way of life but it would start us off far above the point where we actually are. It seems only concerned with the splendid daring and the magnificent prospects of the snow fields and summit precipices when we are still at a loss as to how to find our way through the tangled forest around the mountain's base. Certainly that is the impression which the Sermon on the Mount generally awakes in our ordinary minds: "Blessed are the Peacemakers, for they shall be called the Children of God"—the sublimest of titles, but how is it to be won in the actual world which claims that all issues must be decided ultimately by war? "Blessed are the trained for they shall inherit the Earth"—what a superb legacy but what an impossible condition attached to its granting, when everyone knows I can't help losing my self-control if anyone insults me. "Blessed are they who hunger and thirst after righteousness"—no doubt, but what if I find I have no appetite for that lofty fare?

This is a very sensible objection and the first

chapter has ventured to suggest that Christ was aware of it and provided for it. His teaching did not start on the fifth floor but from ground level. We have only thought this—have only imagined that he was demanding impossible heroics from us "average sensual men," that he had overlooked that we are paralyzed sinners—because we have thought very little of the actual method whereby he would cure and mobilize us, not enough to give it an adequate trial or even to have much verbal knowledge of it.

The life of prayer has seemed to most of us an exploded process. And that is so not merely for those of us who find a strong cocktail better calms our nerves, or a love affair better drives off our depression, or making a packet of money better assuages anxiety than thinking of eternity, or that making a scoop success at our job better takes the edge off life's futility than does the hope of seeing God. Men whom we hold to be thinkers and whom we believe to have looked into the question with detached and expert study have decided that there is really nothing in prayer. Prayer for the puerile: aspirin for adults. Prayer is an escape-mechanism, a childish fantasy-trick, a degenerate form of "sympathetic magic" whereby we run away and try to hide from Reality, telling ourselves that the dark and the bogey man are not really there. We want to believe in a friendly Father—a child complex—and we want thereby to be saved from getting hurt or even from having to dirty our hands with the mud, blood, sewage, and pus of actual life, fecund and festering.

"But prayer sometimes works." That objection used to check for a moment the liquidators of religion. But now they have their answer ready: "Autosuggestion." That phrase has stopped more thoughtful people from praying than perhaps any other single word and, what is even worse (for their prayer must have had very little experience to be so stopped), has stopped most of these people from making any further inquiry into the nature and the effects of prayer. Yet obviously it is no more than a question; it is not a conclusion. The term autosuggestion raises at once a further question—indeed two, and each leads to real knowledge about prayer. The first is the practical one. The critic has now yielded something; he has shifted his ground and withdrawn from his first uncompromising, wholly "debunking" position. He now owns that there is something in prayer, though it is not what those who pray believe it to be. And it is something producing results which the user fails to produce otherwise. That brings us to the question: What is it? The critic maintains that it is not and cannot be anything outside the individual himself. Yet it is something which works for the individual as he cannot work himself. This is certainly so queer a proposition that the question cannot be left there. If it is only *self*-suggestion, why then the need of all this sham and roundabout? Why and how can a pretense, a lie, produce actual results better than a straightforward making-up of one's own mind and giving one's own word to oneself? The fact is that it does, and this empirical fact shows that somewhere in the seemingly simple explanation "only autosuggestion" there must be a catch, a misuse of terms. It is obvious that the whole question turns on what is the "auto." That word "self," it becomes plain, is being used for two profoundly different entities and it is also being used to suggest that, in spite of quite different results, these entities are really the same single person. "Nothing outside the self" is not a definition which helps us at all to solve this strange, pressing problem. The self, our consciousness, is not a spatial thing with a physical inside and outside. The problem we have fallen on here is nothing less than the prime problem of all knowledge, of epistemology: "What am I and what is all the rest?" Every student of the mind has now to acknowledge that there is present with me, unknown even to me, another consciousness, a consciousness the limits and powers of which are radically different from those of my own ego-consciousness, but which can be contacted and which may put its extraordinary powers at my disposal if I know the methods whereby it may be approached. Further, those who have most patiently and unprejudicedly examined the mind are least inclined to say where its upper limits lie and how far outside and above our ordinary selves may stand the power terminals to which, in intense concentration and undistracted attention, we may have access.

Still the standard psychiatrists are holding that

prayer is a fairly useless procedure, not an adult technique, limited in its uses, subject easily to grave abuses and any such benefits as its practice may bestow, able to be obtained in purer form by more modern procedures and treatments. This judgment is quite natural, for two reasons. In the first place their studies have lain almost entirely with those who in this vital respect were subnormal. True prayer, the prayer which produces the most unmistakable and distinctive results, depends first and foremost on power of attention. Psychiatrists have formed their opinion of human nature from two sources. The first is that which is at the disposal of each one of us, the normal man whose power of attention bears exact relationship to his activity. His attention is *held* by what is going on around him. When nothing is happening he daydreams. His power of real attention, of *holding* his mind, is therefore quite low, though he may keep himself interested and active by continually being attracted by outer events. The second and special source of the psychiatrists' knowledge of human nature is the study of his patients. These are people who have failed even to have their minds held by outer happenings and so have sunk into a world of uncontrolled fantasy. Their quality of "mental muscle," of attention, is therefore even lower than that of the average man. In consequence the psychiatrist does not realize that there may be a quality of attention, a power of mental focus, as much above the normal man's as is his above the neurotics. When on his remedial work the psychiatrist has had to go below the surface of the self-conscious mind he has driven his gallery into the hinterland of consciousness. There at some depth he has found a shaft at right angles, perpendicular to his gallery which enters on the level. He has peered down into the depth and has seen below, milling around, the primal urges that run the body. This was a big discovery and often very pertinent to his search—to find out why the individual had gone queer. But the psychiatrist omitted to explore the shaft with full scientific curiosity. It goes up as well as down. Of course in the neurotic it is often blocked above and gaping below. But if normal people are studied the shaft is found partly open at both ends. Further studies of supernormal people show that the shaft is continually opening above; it is a gateway into another quality of consciousness, more intense and also of far wider range.

This brings us to the second reason why the psychiatrist, who is, we must remember, for most of us the final judge as to the mental and spiritual life, thinks the life of prayer an unsatisfactory way of living. The more informed of such physicians of the mind have read the standard studies of religious experience and do not dismiss mysticism as erotic nonsense. But they point out that the results of this method are very mixed and that the whole subject lends itself to fantastic abuse. The real case of the thoughtful man against prayer is not that it is vain but that it is undesirable, a bad way of doing a good thing, a mistaken method for attaining a real improvement. Now with that half-truth the saint, the man who has worked his way through prayer, would agree, while urging strongly that, as with all half-truths, it must not be used straightaway but that the other half must be found before a final judgment can be issued. Today we are almost in the condition, on this important issue, that would obtain if all the pitchblende of the world were in the hands of aborigines, who used raw lumps sometimes to heal and sometimes to damage deeply and sometimes with no result at all, and if all the extracting apparatus were in the hands of those who never had in their hands one ounce of pitchblende or knew, save by wild travelers' tales, where it might be mined. In such a state of things research in radium would not progress, especially if the natives who worked cures said that at no cost must the savants be allowed to test and extract and the savants replied that at no cost must any attempt be made to trace to their sources these strange cases of sporadic powers and cures. Prayer and guidance, which is the product of prayer—as tumor reduction is a resultant of radiotherapy—are both essentially real things but because they are real things they can do real harm and lead to grave mistakes if they are not understood.

In short we may say that piecing together our present knowledge, no unbiased researcher can any longer doubt the following findings: First, our common-sense, casual apprehensions do not give us direct contact with Reality. Those apprehensions— our *sensa*, the messages of which reach us from the outer objective—are not merely heavily censored by our senses before they reach us; they are even more heavily edited by our wishes, assumptions, prejudices. Second, there are ways whereby through learning to pay careful attention, to wait, and to observe in alert passivity, we can have apprehensions which are so powerful and clear that we cannot doubt they come much nearer to Reality than our ordinary, casual, conventional impressions. But third, most people, having obtained such an impression, having received so much clearer an apprehension of Reality than the casual do, once more repeat the mistake of the casual. They, too, become quite certain that they now have absolute access to Reality; they see it as it is. Their impressions they therefore now take as final, as plenary information. If they would recall their past development they would be saved this grave mistake. What stands in the way of the common-sense man, keeping him from seeing the world, say, with the vividness of one of the great impressionist masters? Just that casual assurance that his immediate unthinking impressions, his careless dull and bored eye can show him all there is visible around him. In other words it is prejudice and the vain assumption that I see what there is to be seen which blinds me to Reality. The cocksure ego is certain that it need not look twice at anything to know all that is needed about it. But if it is the assertive ego which blinds us and is always blinding us, are we certain that when we have won a little insight we have wholly got rid of that obliquity of vision? Something real is experienced or has been experienced, but so long as I have in me any self-will I must take care and view my impressions with humble reserve. That ego will and must distort what I see. As astronomers do, I must continually "calculate for displacement," for the fact that because of my situation the star I see, though it undoubtedly is real, is certainly not exactly as I see it. And I have to allow for another grave difficulty from which astronomy is free. Because it is myself, my ego, which distorts what I see, the more pleased I am with myself at my insight, and the more original a finding of my own it appears to be, by so much I must know that my impression is distorted and unreliable.

Now we seem to have reached something very like a vicious circle. The more certain I am, the more certain it is that I am mistaken. There is, however, a way out of this difficulty. It is a way, too, which explains the difficult problem of guidance—how some people obtain what they honestly if hastily believe to be infallible information and instruction but which when acted on proves false. We have seen that it is the presence of the ego which causes these mistakes—the ego with its subtle demands and unceasing, profound needs. No question is more immediate and urgent than: How are we to prevent that deep vigilant force from betraying all our efforts after vision and discrediting all our desire to know Reality? There is only one way, but it is well proved: Let us seek first to be empty of any desire save to know Reality, even of the desire which says Reality must be like our hopes, our dreams; let us resolve above all else to be free from wanting our own way, to be free of desiring to be given a stirring message with which to return, with which to reassure ourselves that others recognize that we have seen; let us determine to wait in a most humbling trust upon utter Being, only believing that He is, not pressing to know how He can be and why He exists or when or whether He will help us. That is the trust, the waiting, the silence of the mouth, which is so anxious to find telling phrases for what it has glimpsed, the silence of the mind, which is so busy imagining what it will see, the silence of the will, which is so impatient to have a schedule and time-table giving the hour when it will arrive; that is the self-naughting. Because it and it alone is sufficiently purgative of the self, it alone prevents the self from distorting what only in such utter silence are we permitted to see. This at last gives true unfailing illumination.

Did Christ hold that view? This prayer seems to show that he did. It shows it by the way it starts. Before we release a force we had best understand its nature. Otherwise we shall do one, or both, of two things. Either we shall fail to make a real contact and give up, maintaining that if there is any result it could be obtained better otherwise. Or we shall touch a force of such power that our apparatus may be wrecked. Our modern minds vacillate between two views, both of them contrary to empirical research, in this vital matter. The one view is that God does not exist. He is simply my subconscious. The other view is that He does exist and I know all about Him, am hail-fellow-well-met with Him. He is constantly at my disposal, as I am, to do what I require. Christ held neither of these views. He maintained that the life of prayer was essential, the only true life, but he also maintained that prayer could not be practiced unless you knew whom you were praying to, what was the nature of the universe in keeping with which you would grow. Most prayer in Christ's day as in ours had in it that initial, disorientating mistake. Men prayed then and pray now without understanding, without trying to understand the Power they addressed. The trouble with those who believed in prayer turns out in the end to be the same as that of those who did not believe in it—neither of them started at the beginning, far enough down. This prayer does not make that mistake. That seems to be the reason why it starts as it does. It begins with a proposition. It begins by defining its terms and by aligning itself to its objective.

Yet what is this definition? "Hallowed be Thy name." What is this? Is this the definition which is to guide us to Reality and to guard us against dangers all the more real because we hardly recognize them? Of all the phrases that run off our tongues in church and in private prayer could we find one more conventional? If a student of religious psychology wanted an expression which would be a perfect example of a speech-reflex in public worship could he find one better? Here, surely, is the standard illustration of a mere sound-pattern to which we attach no meaning and, further, which we believe can have no meaning. We smile at the child who, visiting Boston and having her prayers heard by her hostess, said, "Cabot be Thy Name," and, on being asked why she so garbled the prayer, answered, "At home we are all Halliwells and so, as here you are all Cabots, I thought it would be more polite to change the name." Yet are we, in our vain repetition, any more rational than that child? Are we not even more senseless? The first phrase of the Lord's Prayer, the prayer which he taught at the instant request of his disciples, the prayer as brief as an S.O.S. message, we dismiss as more meaningless than the conventional courtesy-question, "How are you?" with which we greet each other and which we never expect to have answered. Nor are we without scholarly excuse for our perfunctoriness. Has not the greatest of the German New Testament critics, Harnack himself, disposed of the phrase as nothing more than a verbal vestige of the Hebrew dread of the sacred name, a propitiatory gesture to ward off the "ill-luck" which any accidental or careless utterance of a magic spell-word may incur?

Yet this word-worn prayer has in it no padding, "gagging," cliché, or rhetoric. It contains just five supremely urgent statements. It is as tensely brief as a message sent from a sinking ship or an isolated force. It is as terse, exact, laconic as a chemical formula for making dynamite. True, it is full of mysteries, dense with meaning, in spite of its apparently platitudinous familiarity. Yet each of its mysterious terms is dealing with a practical, urgent need; as practical and urgent as breathing and heart-beat. The prayer is concerned throughout with the few supremely important things-to-be-done. It is the briefest of all agendas for immediate action.

But if it is really so urgent and so condensed why then start, and waste time, with a salutation? God does not require to be praised, complimented, to have Himself reminded of His greatness. This most mysterious prayer starts as it does, I believe, for anything but a conventional reason. Indeed it so begins for a reason which, when we come upon it, is positively shocking to our complacency. It so begins because we do not believe in God. Even we who pray are, most of us, at heart quite vague as to the Nature we are addressing. Our complete casualness when supposedly in the Presence proves our fundamental atheism. "That can't be true," we may reply, "For, if I don't believe in God, then what am I doing here praying? Why am I praying at all?" A moment's inquiry will show us a dozen reasons, all of which distract us from true prayer, all of which expose our real unbelief. Look at a few. "I am praying because everyone else is doing so: we rumble away as a flock of sheep stumble and ramble; as a cartful of stones overset jostle and roll down a slope. After all, we are all doing it together and, if it is little use, it can do no harm. Psychotherapeutists say it may even do some good every now and then to relax and wool-gather in harmless company." That is Lie Number One.

Prayer does harm if we do it wrongly. It does harm because it is a real thing, and every real thing used wrongly does harm. If you, in a submarine, are continually "fooling" about with the valves, levers, and bolts of the conning-tower hatch, you may find one day, when you need desperately to work that essential exit, that you cannot do so.

That brings us to the second common reason for praying: "Well, I am praying because it may, after all, do some vague, inexplicable good." That is the "mascot," "phylactery," magic reason. It is Lie Number Two and is even more serious than the first. We have to take great care here. At this point lies a danger, a grave danger, against which this first clause of the Lord's Prayer is specifically set to guard us. Prayer sinks to being a charm. We mean to use it but intend not to understand it too well. Then one of two evil things happens. In the first place we become completely mechanical. Suddenly pressed, like the murderer King Claudius in *Hamlet*, we turn to seek help and find we cannot even ask it.

> My words fly up, my thoughts remain below—
> Words without thoughts never to heaven go.

We are like a man with numbed fingers trying in agony, in vain, not to let a life line slip through his grasp. Or, without that appalling load of evil on our hearts, we may, after years of harmless but useless, degenerative comfort, suddenly find ourselves caught, trapped. Then we turn upon God with a sudden passion. He simply must save us, or those whom we love. For what else has He been there in the background all the time! What is His purpose, meaning, use, but to save us, to save me and mine. We are in an agony. We rouse all our strength. We have never troubled to learn anything of God's nature—no, not even of our own nature and of its mysterious ties with the universe. If our pain is keen enough, our egotism strong enough, our will desperate enough, we may pray with such peremptoriness of demand, such a terrible totality of desire, such a blind and insatiable determination to get our way that our way may be given us, our will may be done—not God's. Because prayer is a real power, because, as has been said, "God were no Creator unless He could create creators," there is a real and terrible danger when prayer is used by people who have been made for the moment single-hearted by an overwhelming desire. They can answer their own prayer and temporarily thwart the Purpose which was working a higher process than they had the selfless power to see. That is why this supreme prayer opens with the great guarding sentences which may be held in one phrase: "Thy Will not mine, be done." Before everything else; before the cramp of heart-breaking sorrow seize me; before I come into the Presence of Power or even rise to singleness of will; not so much for Thy glory (which is above my understanding and indeed, until I have been taught, above my desire) but for my own sake and safety, Thy will be done.

The third common and false reason for praying is the commonest today among socially minded people, ourselves. It is a modern form of prayer. We pray because it pleases God, and by that we do not mean that we are so uneducated as to think there is any real Being to be pleased by our attention or attentive to our pleasure and sorrow. God is just good will. He is the vague spirit of fellowship and philanthropy, of humanitarianism and uplift, whereby we get on with our friends and plan for the poor. He has no inherent existence; He is not *per se*. He is not even merely an appanage, an organ of the universe. He is no more than a state of mind, a reciprocal emotion which we generate of ourselves for ourselves. As an objective fact He is actually less existent, less real than the wax which the bees self-generate out of themselves by clustering together. For the wax is a fact, a material which will remain if and when the bees are killed. But who of us really believes, as clearly as we believe that hive wax is actually on our plate when the bees made it are smoked dead, that God exists and will exist whether we live or die, that the world could vanish and we perish and yet He would exist in His utter completeness and all creation exists simply and solely in Him?

> Though Earth and Man were gone,
> And Suns and Universes cease to be,
> And Thou wert left alone,
> Every existence would exist in Thee!

That, of course, is well-known poetry, and just because it is sonorous we know as a matter of fact that it is simply a figure of speech. Of course it must be. For, if it were real, if we really took these words at even half their face value, how very strange our lives would become, how utterly different the world would look, how radically changed would be our behavior, our conduct, for instance toward our bodies, our possessions, and our positions. Because we simply don't believe in God Himself, a belief which is completely cardinal in the Lord's Prayer, because we think of Him, at most, as a water tank of social service, into which, by our prayers and religious behavior or by coming together and listening to soothing music and sitting about during sedative speaking, we pump a few drops of surplus good will and out of which we and our fellows may draw when we need drive—for this sorry reason and mistake we fall into a worse one. As God is nothing but the Ideal (which is precisely the un-Real) because he is only a value, not a reality; and because he is the dream of gentle lovingness which is quite alien and absent from the actual factual world, he sinks to becoming a moral problem. He is beauty, love, and truth. But of course these are not real things, not even real necessities without which life ends: they are spiritual luxuries. He, then, is not BEING, and as He and his attributes have no actual existence, He cannot defend them or Himself, or rule how they are to be defended, or, finally even rule that they and He shall not be suspended *sine die*, like civil liberties and other social luxuries during a crisis, an emergency, or a war—indeed, whenever we choose to think that spiritual luxury cannot be afforded.

This, then, the third lie about prayer, turns, we see, into the most deadly of them all. That is, we know, the nature of the half-truth lie, always the most deadly because, not being entirely illusion, it launches us on fatal action. The old-fashioned mistakes about prayer—the misapprehensions which make us assume that it either does no harm, or might, perhaps, do us a little good when all other practical helps have failed to get us our way —these mistakes are private mistakes. But the third mistake leads straightway to world calamity. The moment I make a mistake, not now about my wishes and will and how to serve them, but about God's actual nature and what He intends for mankind, disaster descends. As soon as I maintain that utter Reality, the supreme and comprehensive Essence, is no more than my dreams of right and fitness, beauty and truth—at that moment I commit that blasphemy which punishes itself by death, that sin against the Holy Ghost which cannot be forgiven because it is the blind denial of fundamental truth, because it is the sin of Lucifer, the claim to be myself the Godhead and therefore permitted to use any means I hold to be necessary. That is why this third mistaken way of praying may today ruin humanity and destroy our species. When I degrade the Godhead to something which requires my protection, when I say that the Essential Being is so faint and vague, dim and subjective, that, as He only exists as the ideals, aspirations, fine thoughts, and fine feelings that float in my mind and the minds of the few who are my equals, He has to be defended by me—if I fail He ceases to exist, and so I must stoop to any method, however hideous, to preserve the eternal beauty; any means, however evil, to save the eternal goodness; any lie, however base, to establish the eternal truth—when I so say and act, then I am mad with just that pride and blinded with that ignorance which creates satanism. Yet this is precisely how we are acting, and must act the moment we deny God's supreme characteristic. That is not His love, His wisdom, or His power. All these are, as the demoded science of theology has always said, great and wonderful as they are, merely products, attributes of His tremendous nature. The supreme characteristic, whereby the soul in awe recognizes the presence of its Source and Goal, of nature's beginning, continuance, and end, is Being, Actuality, Reality, so intense, so overwhelming, so comprehensive, so searchingly, incessantly immanent, so incomprehensibly transcendent, that we can only conceive of Him as the timeless, illimitable Light, in which for an instant spins the dim speck of the entire temporal universe.

With all his narrowness the Hebrew did avoid this pathetic impertinence—the impertinence of patronizing the Creator, of an ephemeral creature taking the Eternal under its protection. The Jew did believe, first and foremost, in God as Being, as Reality. True, our Lord teaches that God is the loving Father of His creation, but this teaching was a revelation of supreme wonder; it was not a platitude. Jesus and his hearers all shared a common conviction about God. It was expressed for them in the words, "No flesh shall see God and live." It is on that tremendous background, we must never forget, on that awful depth of God's utter Beingness, against that intensity of the Eternal, that Christ throws his revelation. We cannot grasp what he meant, indeed we must fall into the ghastly error into which the churches and so many Christians have fallen today, unless we understand, as he and all his generation understood without question that God is of such utter reality that He is more terrific, more awe-inspiring than any other thing or being, than the entire visible universe, than the highest attainment of good, than the deepest horror of evil. For all these things are faint, fleeting, and shadowy beside that. None can approach such intensity of Being, and to begin to conceive of it is to have the first suspicion of what awe can be.

So we need, we who are being whirled in hopeless vertigo by the centrifuge of time, in order to orientate ourselves toward the Eternal, to begin our prayer with complete recognition of the Nature to whom we are addressed. That first clause tells us the key in which this prayer is to be prayed; it is an indication of the carrying-wave in which any message from time to eternity must be transmitted. Because we have been so glib with the name of God, the reality has faded out of it and we are left believing in nothing but a shadowy good will, a gentle decency, to defend which moderate ideals we soon find ourselves compelled actually to outrage them utterly. Before, then, we can win to that height of vision where we dare say as fact, and not as an amiable lie, "God is Love," we must have learned the lessons of hard reality that stand in our path up the purgatorial mountain, and that until they are faced, forbid our facile phrase adding to anything but general despair. "Thou shalt not take the name of the Lord thy God in vain." We have taken that name in vain—we have blasphemously attached it to the prospectus of nationalistic ambitions and imperialistic adventures, to class privileges, revolutionary campaigns, community causes, personal passions. God is not mocked. Because He did not make a human protest or display resentment, we mistook His patience for indifference and soon, when an indifferent God seemed an expense of time and an obstacle to reason—an otiose hypothesis—we took this apparent lack of righteous anger and proper pride as a proof of His nonexistence. The penalty for mocking God, for real blasphemy—not childish slips of the tongue and verbal foolishness, but those serious, grave, prepared misstatements about His nature, misstatements far more often found in the mouths of bishops than of bandits—that penalty still stands, as inescapable as natural law, for it is natural law.

The outcome is given by the Hebrew in anthropomorphic language: "They shall call, and I will not answer." Hell, the mystics have always told us, is nothing but the utter absence of any sense of God, the complete conviction that He is nowhere. And we reflected privately. After all, was the worst place no worse than that? Surely that is not so bad. We could think of being far more uncomfortable, and, though of course it would be better, more respectable, more romantic to have the old aura of the ideals somewhere gilding the horizon, still if we have to be denied all that, we might learn to get on somehow without that atmosphere. But we cannot get on without Being, without any reality. Quite soon, as in a sunken submarine, the invisible but essential air gives out, becomes tainted, deadly, as life today is becoming dense with fumes in Europe and no one knows any longer quite clearly what is true and what life means and why it is worth living. Ideologies—for which one must die and suffer torment, for which one must sacrifice compassion as a debilitating vice and truth as a "bourgeois lie" and humanity as "democratic nonsense"—these idols to which everything which makes life happy and worthy were to be sacrificed, themselves are turned upside-down in a night. No one who is sensible can believe any "news," for lying is loyalty. No one can still believe for no one can be sure that he will not be commanded to reverse his faith tomorrow. Can reason hold, can life endure in such an atmosphere? Is not this hell?

It is when this process which is now spreading round the globe reaches a pitch already attained in many countries that we begin to gasp, but our lungs take in no breath of life. Now we want to believe but can't. Because we have mocked God, have known in our hearts that He was unreal, have known that He was merely the propaganda label to plaster over the contraband we wished to smuggle past the still-stirring, still-anxious conscience of mankind, have degraded our thought of Him to suit our convenience, our penalty is sure. We are caught, trapped: our side is failing, our desperate shifts and means, our mixed motives, double purposes, ambiguous alliances, secret treaties, our whole policy and plan is going down in confusion and defeat. We cry out in our agony—and no answer comes. "They shall cry and I will not harken." The penalty of saying that we believe in God and of showing by our acts that we do not is just this: We are taken at our exact word. God is merely an ideal to be shifted and served as conditions and conveniences dictate. God is the resonant peroration with which, when enemies are crushed and we are undisputed master, we justify our rule, our strong, stern, necessary methods and our future program of enduring dominance. We assert that we could not have succeeded had not the universe chosen us, and because, therefore, we are the manifest product of destiny we must not be weak, tolerant, or kind or spare anyone. That would be failing our high calling, "through craven fear of being great." It is, we then conclude in a tumult of applause, God's will, which we dare not thwart, that we not merely crush opposition but put under us as serfs forever those "lesser breeds without the Law," who dared oppose God in us. That, of course, is the creed for victory, stereotyped for all war propaganda which has to be addressed to the religious—those who still need the name of God as an alibi for acts from which the normal conscience still revolts. Of course it was always blasphemy, but when we have committed it nothing awkward seems to have happened and the queasy consciences of the over-scrupulous were silenced. Very well. "But the end is not yet." *Respice finem.* There comes an hour for every individual, yes, and for every community, an hour when everything we can do for ourselves, every means we can twist to our ends, has failed and we are sinking inexorably into the gulf of utter blackness. There comes that hour when we would give all that we have and are for one gleam, for one sign that God is, in Himself, not the luxury of an ideal, but the necessity of a fact. We cry, and only the silence answers.

Again the old harsh working wisdom of mankind counsels us while we still have time, "Seek Him when He may be found, for in the great floods thou shalt not come nigh Him." Crude, but sternly practical. We are not fit yet for the gospel. For us, with our terrible insincerity, the only thing we can really understand is law. We sentimentalize the good news and the deadly danger of sentiment is precisely this, that it is quite insincere; it likes warm words and never believes that they refer to real things, more real than agony and death. Sentimentality is the commonest escape from life, the shiftiest treason to truth. That is why it is always found in company with the coldest cynicism. Evil, whose home is the hell of complete unreality, has no more effective decoy. Our Lord taught, as the greatest discovery that he could give mankind, that we might hope to find and face God. We have taken his daring formula and have framed it as a pretty text which looks well on nursery walls. The Law remains: "No flesh shall see God and live." No creature still ruled by its self-will, no ego determined still to get its own way, if necessary by saying it is really God's way, the best way of saving God, no individual still motivated by greed and fear, by excitement and anxiety, by self-centeredness, shall see God and live.

We should note the terms of the sentence exactly. The words are as precise as a sentence by a judge or the operational diagnosis of a surgeon, lancet in hand. The judgment does not say, "No flesh shall see God," and leave it at that. No, it is a graver matter for our slipshod selves. We cannot avoid God, we cannot escape Reality. We hide, but find that terror and dread of that Unknown we would not know is with us in our hiding place— "When Me they fly I am the Wings." "No flesh shall see God and live." Nothing can save us from that meeting. There is no middle way of hanging between life and death. To delay that meeting, because it seems too awful is only to make it more awful. What is the world doing today, what is its agony, but its meeting with Reality and its struggle to deny that Reality is confronting it? That being our fate, our destiny, the reason for our creation, what are we to do about it? It is here that we begin to see why Christ's words are a real gospel. There is no inevitable spiritual progress. Simply by going on living we are carried always closer to Reality, that is true, but we do not become one whit more able to recognize this fact; on the contrary, unless we make constant effort we become less and less able to realize the true nature of our situation. We become more and more certain that the whole thing is a ghastly muddle and we ourselves have had a foul deal. This world is now giving us a monster demonstration that hell is not a fancy created solely by those disordered brains which are confined to asylums. Hell is loose now over half the world and the flame is spreading. Hell is a fact; it is the condition which men, who will not face God and yet by their nature cannot escape Him, must precipitate. If we remain self-obsessed creatures we shall confront God, whom we shall only be able to recognize as unbearable Reality. The Real then appears as the utterly senseless, the too horrible to be believed, as we say "the impossible," what makes absolute nonsense of all our reasons for living. But there it stands, right across our path, across our horizon. It is Reality surely enough, but because of what we have been, because of the lies we have spoken and lived, we cannot face it. We cannot face it, deny it, or avoid it. Unable to accept or understand and yet unable to deny the fact of our experience, we shall endure that horror of hopelessness which is hell, we shall face two conflicting experiences, the matter of fact and the matter of meaning, a world of facts which outrage all meaning and, as we are incapable of reconciling these two demands, the very basis of our being will be torn in two.

This is no fancy forecast. The last few months the scientific journals have been featuring the discovery that even rats, confronted with a situation which they see they must solve but to which their sense and experience only give them replies which leave them still caught, under this shock of complete frustration fall into mental collapse. But this ending is for us not inevitable. It will happen if we do not act, but it need not happen if we will act on the guidance we have been given. The single-hearted, those who here and now would do one thing, would find Reality and seek one Being whose manifestation is understanding love, these seek and find, their eyes open and they see God, they die to themselves, are consumed in that Light and are reborn. Those who have desired just this one thing; who have known themselves, as they find themselves, to be desperately, grotesquely inadequate; who have known that they cannot solve the world's agony; no, not that of those they love or even their own inner conflict—such a humility, such a sincerity, such an unrestricted, unlimited casting of the self into the deep of God's being, such an act and such only, finds Him. This is today no vague gesture, nor the expression of a nihilistic pantheism. Unless we can plunge through the blazing wreckage of our hopes, our ideals, our sense of order and progress, our notions of decency and humanity, we shall die, like wretched horses rooted with panic in a burning stable. But if we will throw away all our inflammable shams and pretenses; if we will dare seek one thing and one thing only—the sheer presence, the constant and complete reality of God—then desperately seeking we shall find and dying behold we live.

It can hardly be done in a moment, but we can begin at once. We can resolve to put aside anything and everything which makes God unreal for us. We can, at this very moment and henceforward without fail, pray with all the sincerity and intensity we can command, "Hallowed be Thy Name." Then day by day that unspeakable Reality will dawn through the phantasmagoria of our present life, and, through the dissolving wreckage of a world which founded itself on a lie—the lie of the unreality of God—will break the splendor of the light of utter Being. That is the only possible guarantee that the world can be saved from its already enforced liquidation. Let no one turn us from this one hope of salvage by telling us that things are not so bad as to demand such drastic effort on our part, or (the other attempt to lure us away from the pumps into the chartroom to look at pictures of distant harbors where a free and happy humanity will ride at anchor) that we should not escape into a morbid interest about the water gaining in the hold. We are told that the ship—human nature, is really all right, only the officers need "liquidation." The ship is sinking because it is not seaworthy. The fault lies below any economic mismanagement—that is a symptom, as is the heeling of a sinking ship. The fault lies in our common human nature, right down in our gaping willful ignorance of Reality, our widening ignorance and disregard of God. If we face that, then at last the ship can be made sound. There is a hope for humanity. The voyage can be continued. Then we shall not founder, for our civilization will rest on Reality, on real sanctions and sense. We shall not drift and be wrecked because we shall have a true compass, clock, sextant, and clear sun and stars to show where we are and whither we should go. Then real advance is possible. Then we may know the truth of those words which follow with the inevitability of law: "Thy Kingdom come on Earth, as it is in Heaven."

III. THE KINGDOM

"Thy Kingdom come; on Earth as in Heaven."

✤✤

This is the second part of the fivefold formula which we are attempting to decode and apply. Let us for a moment recall what we have already been able to define. We have made out the key in which the whole of this composition is meant to be played—the carrying-wave in which the whole of this transmission is conveyed from the eternal to the temporal. That basis is that God is Reality, utterly greater, far more real than anything else. Everything else, everyone else, all objects and persons are merely phenomena, appearances, more or less permanent in so far as they are near or far from that Center. He and He alone is absolutely real. Of this axiom we need remind ourselves, because, in religion, we are so slipshod with words. That statement about deity is not the language of devotion, still less of adulation. It is simply the terminology of accurate, painstaking, scientific thinking. The world and our physical selves are phenomena and there is some tremendous Reality underlying and sustaining this transitory appearance of things. About God's goodness, about God's usefulness in getting us our way, physics knows nothing, but it does know about a stupendous reality, beyond all power of imagining, underholding all. If we wish to speak clearly and think accurately and not use words uselessly but to describe things as they are, then we have to say that Reality, what actually is, is quite different from that world of temporary construction, misconception, and fantasy in which we all, except the single-hearted, choose to stay—whether we are practical men making a pile, or "power types" satisfying a blind urge to domination or simply frank sensualists in search of a soothing, detensioning sensation.

We must then keep that first statement in mind, because this following clause depends wholly on its predecessor. Perhaps we had better repeat the actual words with which we are now concerned, "Thy Kingdom come, Thy Will be done on Earth as it is in Heaven." If we do not keep the precise wording in mind, we are very likely, nowadays, to overlook the fact that the prayer, in this second clause, has still not said anything about us, either as beneficiaries or as helpers. The prayer is addressed to the absolute Reality and asks Him to manifest His will in this dim, less-real world of time, as that will is eternally actual in heaven. We may not believe that there is such a Reality and such a place where He is wholly manifest. It is indeed much to believe and anyone who comes really so to believe finds his life curiously and radically altered. But what we must accept is the fact that that is what this prayer says and its composer did believe. Because it is so hard to believe that there is a Reality, beside which this world is but a shadow (though a significant and pressing shadow), and because such a belief must change all our lives—our view of our personalities, our possessions and our appetites—we therefore are inclined to change this clause quite considerably in our minds. Because for so many of us God is not absolute Reality but simply our good will, simply ourselves when we feel well intentioned, we render this clause, as a matter of fact, not as it stands. When we pray it we really mean: "Give *us* the power to bring in Thy Kingdom," or even, "Give us leave to bring in Thy Kingdom by whatever means we may find necessary."

We must then repeat: Because this prayer believes in God as the only complete Reality, because of that fact, it asks *Him* to bring in His Kingdom. It is in His power and His alone to cause this thing to be. Then why does He not do so? What precisely are we doing here, asking Him to act? Does He not wish His Kingdom to be on earth? What is our part in this fundamental transaction, this the only real revolution? Cannot we help? Cannot we co-operate with that divine event, "the restoration of all things"? We have certainly thought we could. Indeed, we went so far as to believe that the Kingdom would and would only be brought in by us. We were "God's hands." Why then all this delay? After two thousand years, quite a span of humanity's entire civilized life, during which the Christian Church has been for most of the time the dominant force among the most active portions of mankind—after all those years and protracted opportunities, the world, certainly at this moment, the year of grace 1940, looks no more like God's Kingdom than it did at the start. Christians are ranged up on almost all of the many active battle-fronts ready to kill one another and, moreover, are convinced that it is God's will that their fellow-Christians the other side of the firing line should be exterminated. As a political force there can be no doubt that Christianity is in eclipse. The most politically powerful of all individual Christians, the pope, does not venture to use the power of moral censure given him to excommunicate the evil while he does dare to use the power vested in him to release his priests from their vow, the vow that as they serve a God who is Truth itself, Who has all power and Who was revealed by His Son as a loving Father, they must not shed their brothers' blood nor use the unlimited violence and cunning of war.

Are we quite helpless? Cannot we co-operate at all in bringing in the Kingdom? Is God waiting for us? Surely he wants us to help? Yes, we are certainly intended to share in that work. But we can only do so on two conditions, two conditions which do much, when frankly examined, to explain the present tragic impasse. The first is obvious, yet it has often been overlooked. We must know, in point of fact, what the Kingdom actually is. We must start with right knowledge: we must know the nature of our objective. There is today a popular impatience with defining our ends precisely. We call that (it is Lenin's phrase) utopianism. True, it may be difficult to say in outward detail what our final goal will be like, but the only people who are free to keep their aim unexpressed are those who are very careful with their means. If you take sufficient care that your means are good your ends will be good. But if you know *that* about your means you know intuitively the essential nature of your end. It is clear that the end will be, first and foremost, a state of being which is supremely good and real, so good and so real that as long as we make use of evil, whose nature must always be bad and false, as long as we have (for whatever reasons and excuses) contact with any evil, we cannot attain that state. That discovery about the end leads us back to the means. We know enough of our goal to know the only means which will take us there, to know that anything less than complete goodness will not take us, but must lead us in the opposite direction, in fact in that direction in which we see the world is going with accelerating speed.

Having discovered the first thing about the Kingdom, we realize that we have to have the right power, the particular, appropriate force which will bring the Kingdom to us and us to the Kingdom. For it becomes clear that these two conditions of right knowledge—of the direction and the objective—and of right power, the apt means, are interrelated. As then we shall only be able to find the power, to aid the Kingdom's establishment among us, if we know as precisely as we may all that can be known about the Kingdom's nature, it is essential that we should discover all that the prayer tells us about that state. This prayer describes the Kingdom; it defines it. The definition is, though, a peculiar one. It is definition by locality. The prayer in its descriptions uses that method. At the beginning, God Himself is not defined as Creator, or Redeemer, or Judge, but by where He is—in heaven. And so in turn His Kingdom is described in the same way. The Kingdom is in heaven—it is the will of God as done in heaven. Now will, in our temporal language, means something we intend, something which we may be at a loss how to effect, generally something in the future. But God's will, which is in eternity, is actuality. What He wills *is*, is absolute Reality. The Kingdom is, then, complete Being, absolute Existence, utter Truth, absolute Awareness, absolute Freedom. It is clear, then, that we must be ourselves in heaven before we can bring heaven around us or to a single person around us. And, it is equally clear, that heaven is no vague rainbow land, a shimmering "interference-fringe" which we let blur the sharp, cruel edges of immediate reality. Heaven is Reality because it is true, even before it is good, for truth is nearer to our conception of what IS than goodness. What is truth? Christ is reported to have replied to Pilate's vexed dismissal of the issue, that it made those who experienced it free. How? By freeing them from the continual fretting tension between what ought to be and what seems in fact to be, between the nobility of our ends and the squalor of our means; by freeing us from the eroding anxiety which, because we are always being torn between our clinging to a fading past and our pursuit of a beckoning, elusive future, wears away our life. As a matter of clear, accurate thinking, truth can only exist when time is overcome. For what is the scientific definition of truth: "Truth is Correspondence." A thing is true when we can exactly repeat it. But how can we, as long as we are in time? "You cannot step twice into the same stream"; that old Greek saying revealed long ago this awkward fact. It has nothing to do with metaphysical theorizing. It is the heart and source of our very grave condition. In time we can never quite tell the truth; what we say and what we do is never quite real. Of our nature, as it is, there is always something unreal and false about us. We approach nearest to truth when our acts and thoughts are nearest to the Timeless, the Eternal. We shall see that this supremely realistic prayer returns to this basic and indeed very terrible problem once and again, until, at the close, this problem and this alone confronts us as the supreme issue and the darkest of mysteries.

Here, then, it must be enough to remind ourselves that what this prayer preaches is that heaven alone is real and that to attain that Reality our first step is to do nothing that denies Reality, even though so to act makes us lose opportunities for giving evil some of its own medicine. The first thing we have to do is to receive Reality right into our natures (and our natures take it up very slowly) in spirit and in truth.

That consideration brings us back to the second requirement if we are to help in bringing the Kingdom: the power needed, the rightful gifts required to establish such a state of being. How can we have the strange force needed to establish such a tremendous thing? It is clear that if the Kingdom is so great, so divine, any of the means which we find at our present disposal can never bring it about. On the contrary, they will simply postpone its coming and drive us further away from it. Too often when we are certain that we are aiming at something good, the more good it is the less careful we feel we need be about our methods, means, and powers. But if the Kingdom is so supremely good, it is certainly clear that to use wrong or even inadequate means is to insure that we shall never enter it. If it is Reality, then to involve ourselves further in lies is surely to depart further from it. The Kingdom, then, cannot be brought in—it can only be driven away—by any use of coercion or of trickery. There are no "white lies," any more than there are really "benignant" cancers. Even organization may be a mistake because we too often like to think that lack of spirit may be remedied, or at least disguised, by increase of apparatus, as though, when we have run out of gas, we could conceal the fact by adding a few more cylinders to the inert engine. And once you have an organization then compromises begin to be made, not merely for the cause, but for the organization itself, not under the excuse of reaching the end, but for the odd reason that the means themselves are somehow sacred. So we find people making compromises, committing crimes for their churches and brotherhoods and parties, compromises and crimes which they say blandly they would never commit for themselves and dare not say they would commit for God. Our Lord evidently held that the Kingdom was not an organization but rather a contagion. It is a state of mind which spreads and forms through our being with those whose lives are so fermenting with this divine "culture," with this "hidden leaven."

Now the first thing which we have to face up to when we have defined the Kingdom and the means to it, the power needed to attain it, is the fact that we have none of this apt, real power. We have plenty of the wrong sort of force: the unlimited violence and cunning of war—which we excuse because it is labeled to be used to create world-brotherhood and to banish war. We have the power of advertising eloquence, which we use to make ourselves feel that we are far better and more effective and real than we know we are. But the real force—not words or violence, but actual spiritual power, the divine indwelling life—that we lack and we and everyone else know we lack. Some shrewd Oxford dons were discussing one day which personage is the more powerful, a bishop or a judge. "The bishop," said one, "for the judge can only say, 'You be hanged,' while the bishop can say, 'You be damned.'" "Ah," replied the other, "but when the judge says 'You be hanged,' you *are* hanged." The same fact, the lack of spiritual power recognized by ecclesiastical authorities, is illustrated by the story of the pope, seated with the great medieval theologian Thomas Aquinas watching the revenues of Europe being carried into the Vatican. He exclaimed, "The time has gone when the Church had to say, 'Silver and gold have I none.'" And the theologian replied, "And the time has also gone when she could say to the paralytic, 'But what I have I give thee, Arise and Walk!'"

Hence, as we really lack any real and right power to bring in the Kingdom, when we confront evil we collapse in one way or the other. Either we truckle and make terms with it, covering our defeat with words, saying we are realists and are saving what can be salvaged out of the wreck. Or we sink to evil's own level in the other way: we own it to be right and real because we use its methods, its means, violence, and cunning, cruelty and deceit, to attempt to check it. Beelzebub cannot cast out Beelzebub. But, as we have no spiritual power with which to exorcise evil, what can we do? The first thing is to be honest: to own our helplessness; to confess that we are bankrupt, paralyzed, pretending to issue money but it is fraudulent, talking big about moving and carrying others with us but really carried wherever the actual forces of the world intend. It is worth recalling Frederick of Prussia's shrewd contemptuous reply when asked why the clergy of his realm were allowed to preach with little state interference: "They say what they like; I do what I like."

We are not free. It is a painful fact to confess, especially in a democracy where we assume that we are all naturally free. But we shall never become free until we own that we are captives. Though, however, we are captives that is not to say that we do nothing. It would be much better if we did nothing. The real trouble is that we imagine we are free and so we are always finding false explanations—rationalizations—to show why what we do is intentional and noble. So, to the captivity of our active life we add the further and damning captivity of our minds and thoughts. That is what Plato rightly and terribly called "The lie of the soul." Once we lie to ourselves our chances of ever finding the truth become very dim indeed. The first thing, then, that we must do, if we would help the Kingdom, is to own that we are incapable. We must, with patient, humiliating honesty, watch ourselves. And then we shall quickly discover (it is so obvious that this has little to do with spirituality; it is a commonplace of rudimentary psychology, which we ought to have mastered before we ever thought of facing up to the life of the soul) that our incessant activity, our busyness, has very little to do with what we say it has. There is very little intention of any sort, however primitive, however self-seeking, about it. We are not even consistently, intelligently selfish. Our actions are mainly conditioned reflexes, things which we do without thought, as to either the means or the ends. We have an itch to be active, for if we were still our minds might begin to ask us awkward questions about ourselves. It is therefore convenient to rush off at every fresh cry and accept the suggestion of every slogan. Our excuses, our rationalizations would not, do not deceive a child of six, but we all have the same profound reasons for wanting to accept them as true. So we swap each others' lies—"You believe my story and I'll believe yours"—for we both have the same awkward fact to hide. Our deeds, our rushings about, if we review the whole of them at one day's end, have little more purpose about them than the random gesturings and twitchings of St. Vitus' dance. But they serve the one grim purpose of keeping us from seeing ourselves. Lao Tzu says, "Muddy water let stand becomes clear," but that clarity is precisely what we want to shun.

What can we do about it? It is clear that it is no use talking about helping to bring in the Kingdom when we discover not merely that we have none of the right power with which it may be brought, but, in point of fact, that we have no power at all, and there is even reason to suppose that we don't want to have any. That is where so many of us who wish to do good have actually been more negative than even the evil. They have power of a sort, and sincerity of a sort. We simply have none, and in desperation at that fact, when they have blackmailed us out of the pretense which we call peace, and we try to imitate them, in war we only do the job worse than they. A rattler is more effective, if it is a lower type, than a twitching paralytic. Once, however, we have the desperate humility to face that fact, we can do something. If we reject that something as being beneath our dignified notion of ourselves, then we shall remain the most helpless of all captives, he who refuses to confess that he is a slave. But if we will own humbly that, as we are, we can do nothing, that we can only harm the Kingdom we would help, then there is a step which can be taken at once toward the way out.

The first thing to realize is how much power, vigilance, alacrity, and skill are required just to stop doing harm. Just by being what we are, active shams pretending to be good, working busily at what our deep heart and mind tell us is deliberate self-illusion, deliberate escape from where the real, dreaded, unsolved problem lies, we go on doing every moment incalculable evil. Why does the world as a whole believe with complete conviction that there is no such thing as powerful, fascinating good—good in its own right, good the natural master before which evil cringes? Mainly because of us. The good, we know, are on the whole ineffective and forbidding when they are not actually hypocrites. The love, joy, and peace, let alone the power and the glory, which should radiate through us, as warmth and light radiate through a clear glass turned to the sun—well, we know the world is right; we radiate about as much as a disconnected heating-pad. For that is precisely our condition: we have no connection with Reality. We are not plugged in; there is no contact. The Kingdom is more thwarted by the hopeless inconsistency of us, who say we stand for it, than by the consistency of the evil who oppose it openly. It is infinitely more discouraging to see how the good fail, to see what they call doing good, than to see how the evil succeed. The true ground for despair is to note what passes and is accepted as goodness—the picked fruits of our chosen leaders—rather than the grimmest estimate of the forces which frankly declare themselves parasites and destroyers. It is the abject standard of psychological health (let alone spiritual power) with which we are content, complacent— we, who think of ourselves as the world's salt. There lies the real gravity of our pass. No wonder when it comes to doing anything practical (such, for example, as creating the sanction for right conduct) our "sanctions" have to be just the same as, indistinguishable from, the evil man's own weapon, unlimited violence and cunning. We talk of spiritual power. The world naturally replies, "Produce it!" And, driven into a corner, we produce what? Just what the world has, and has always known and is now going to the devil with: propaganda, lies, the devil's own language, and violence, his native weapon. If we turn a moment from the Kingdom and the openly hostile forces which stand in its path, and face ourselves, who are the force to bring it in, are any words more apt and true to describe us than those of that old realist the Duke of Wellington, when he viewed the new recruits rushed out to save his armies: "I don't know what impression they will make on the enemy: I know they fill *me* with terror!"

Yet raw troops can become hardened veterans if, before thinking of victory, they first train. Soldiers cannot afford not to be realists. They have little use for emotions, enthusiasm; they build on the rock and foundation of the reflexes and until they have dug down to that level they refuse to lay a single stone. We have to learn from them. When Hannibal marched all round Rome, the citizens called for action—and found disaster. Then it was that Fabius Maximus, not afraid to be dubbed the Cunctator, the Delayer, won the right to command the legions and freed Italy, wearing down his opposed genius by refusing to be drawn into premature battle. When King Charles of England was exhausting the parliamentary forces, Cromwell, likewise, gained leave to decline action until he had built up his New Model army. Then, in two actions, he broke the king. When the Samurai rose against the new modernized Japanese government in the sixties of the last century, the government almost despaired. But, once again, true advice said, "Discipline can be learned," and within a few months the imperial army, though having to use peasants and opposed by the native discipline of the Samuraï, nevertheless brought them to their knees.

We must lay off from our proud schemes of putting the world under our control as God's vicegerents. We must resist the false alliance offered us by the powers of this world when they say, "all you have to do is to lend your name and inspire the young to this or that crusade and you shall have half-profits when we win." We have to deny ourselves the glad feeling that here and now we can win the world for God by striking in when a sudden crisis flares and people cry, "For Gawd's sake *do* something!" We have to own that that decision was settled long ago. When we could have affected the future, we were idle or lazy or blind. The day of opportunity is past. Now all we can do is in bitter humility to learn not to let opportunity slip again, when it will recur, for "No man is free at the moment of action." We must then, first and foremost, self-train. That means much. It means unstitching what has been illstitched; deconditioning what has been idly and wrongly conditioned. Increasingly, physical trainers are finding that the first step which one who is crooked must take if he would become straight is to inhibit the old ways. He must stop, he must hold up every action and become again conscious of what he is actually doing as though he were doing it for the first time in his life. He can't alter it yet, but he can become aware of it; how wrong, inefficient and futile it is. He can ask, Why do I do that? The answer comes: Because you are not free. You dream. You flatter yourself that you are free. In point of fact you are an automaton, and every year, indeed by every action, you are becoming more and more of a machine. This is a serious but *not* a despairing answer. In fact, by asking the question the first small area of freedom has been cleared from the encroaching bind-weeds of habit. And as we watch and note, we find that that area of freedom, like dawn over a dark landscape, spreads; we see clearer and farther down into the depths and sources of action. The blind impulses, first seen for what they are, now, in turn, begin to weaken and hesitate and finally to wait for our order. We find, by owning we had no power but to watch helplessly our unintentional behavior, that power has actually flowed back to us and we are in truth master of our own house.

That is why it is necessary, however hard, that we stop what we are actually doing—thwarting God's Kingdom, the Kingdom of freedom and creative power and complete consciousness. It was pure wishful dreaming that made us think we were forwarding it. We cannot forward it as we are; and as we are we shall use every subterfuge, even that of saying we are God's hands and so far too busy and important to think or pause, to prevent our recognizing what we are—obstacles to the Kingdom. We must start without delay on the painful, steep, humiliating path of undoing our busy, deliberately deluded selves. So only will the Kingdom come, where it must come fully and where we alone can decide whether it shall come—in ourselves. "The Kingdom of God is within you," yes, but only if we are prepared to let that powerful germ of eternal life grow, until it splits away and consumes this husk, our ego. Unless we, this person with his tightly bound triple self-love—love of his physical appetites and comforts, of his possession, of his place, rank, and recognition—unless that hard and hardening nut is buried and rots and is eaten away by the new life's germ, there is no hope. Indeed we may say that the whole secret of the spiritual life is just this painful struggle to come awake, to become really conscious. And, conversely, the whole process and technique of evil is to do just the reverse to us: to lull us to sleep, to distract us from what is creeping up within us; to tell us that we are busy workers for the Kingdom when we are absent-mindedly (while we daydream of our importance) spreading death, not life; to persuade us that we are wise, practical, creative, when we are sinking daily into a blinder and more fatal automatism.

That, then, is the first step, known by the grim technical term, purgation. I must start with myself, and stay with myself until some intention appears in my actions, some consistency between what I say and do. I must not escape into denunciation, coercion, or even superior concern for anyone else. I shall do so if I can; that is the invariable trick of the ego, trying to escape and save itself from its necessary death. "When God turns on man, man turns on his neighbor," said old Jeremy Taylor some three centuries ago. Then, after that complete abandonment of serving two masters—my view of myself as a master-builder gaining recognition by my active goodness, and of God—then comes the next step, illumination. I am still far below being capable of a creative act. That is God's prerogative, and He gives it only to those who have given themselves away that He may occupy the space they once filled. But I am permitted at last to see things as they are. Fear and hurry and anxiety leave me. Why? Because, though still extremely ignorant, I know one thing at last. I know that God exists. There is utter Reality, complete creative power holding the entire creation in its grasp. The whole of time and space is no more than an incident, a minute episode in the immeasurable order, power, and glory of complete Being. Once I have seen, really seen, that, once I am illuminated, then I have fully attained one step in approaching God's Kingdom and in letting it approach; I no longer am standing in the way. I cease to bar the Light. I cease to be a reason for people not believing in God. The Light shines through those who have so opened themselves, or rather let themselves be opened. Thank God we have all of us known one or two of them. And there may be more of them than we notice, for they are the reverse of showy. They may be very active, but when we think of them it is not of their activity, physical or mental, of which we think. It is of some still, firm quality, some essence deeper than deeds, that we see in them. They see Reality, are always looking at it, and, through that seeing, there is in them a quality of entire Being.

Is there anything beyond that stage? That is indeed much; but does not the world's present pass call for even more? Yes, if we wish it, there is a still higher degree. We have found the beginning of a way leading to the Kingdom of Eternal Life. First, there is the death of the self, the unlearning of our wrong ways. Then there is the radiation of the germ which has cast its husk. After we have abandoned self, we may see what the Kingdom is.

The first stage is that of servantship, when we learn not to disobey. The second stage is one of friendship, when we learn why we have had to obey, and to abstain from much that seemed harmless and even, in its way, right. A servant knoweth not what his master doeth. A friend is shown the plan, and his clear conviction that he has seen and the manifest effect which his vision has had on his life, help him to trust that there is a purpose, to endure and to obey. Then comes the third stage, that of creative action, the station and work of sons. These may be intrusted with the creative power, because their whole wills and consciousness are God's. They are not merely illuminated; they are united. They are not merely privileged onlookers, they are coworkers. This is the well-known (but seldom climbed) ladder of the mystics. But let us look at it again, not dismissing it as a rare path reserved for ecstatics. Is it not also, here in front of us today, unmistakably, an evolutionary path, the evolutionary path, the Way of Life for all? Is not this the way to the Kingdom and is not the attainment of that final station itself the Kingdom? To some people this may seem something of an anticlimax. Is the dream of the Kingdom to end simply with the ivory-tower ideal of a large crop of saints? If we think that goal anything less than the highest, that can be because we have never met any of that highest third rank—as well may be. They are themselves rare and, moreover, like all supreme masterpieces, those who would understand them must in themselves have already something of the nature they would appreciate. If we are quite blind, however intense the sun, we shall still see only darkness. We cannot be illuminated by any increase of the radiation; we can only be burnt. And should anyone during the night tell us of the sun we dismiss such tales as foolishness. For sainthood in such degree is something more than lofty character. The Sons of God differ from us not only in character but in capacity. They are not merely good and wise but theirs is of the essential nature of their Father, a quality, an intensity of Being, which is, unless they screen it from us, disquieting, uncanny. Real creativeness is far more terrible than what we call destruction.

Can we ourselves hope to climb this tremendous way to the Kingdom? Certainly: we are called, all of us, to do so. Certainly: there will be no Kingdom unless and until we do so climb to that station. For only those who have attained may safely be given the powers, the spiritual powers whereby, and only whereby, God's Kingdom may come on earth. How can we learn to climb to such immense heights? We have seen the first steps. The very first is to know that I as I am, am an obstacle to the Kingdom. I must start, before anything else, by clearing myself out of the way. I must learn, right down to my reflexes, to say and mean and know, "Let my name perish, so Thy Kingdom come." I must grasp the purging truth in the austere sayings, "He who would love God truly will not expect God to love him," and "He who loves God as God should be loved, loves Him without fear and without hope." And then? Then we are ready for the next clause in this master-prayer—the first clause to mention us. We have given up all assurance and hope in ourselves. And yet we are set to achieve a purpose and power beside which all human achievement looks puny. How can we do that? We have seen that we first must and can empty ourselves. It is the next petition, asking at last something for us, which reveals how we may be filled, fed, and so raised in our evolution that we may be possessed of the divine power, and thus, and thus only, help bring in the divine kingdom, "On Earth as it is in Heaven."

IV. THE BREAD

"Give us this day the Bread of the Coming Day."

❖❖❖❖❖❖❖❖❖❖❖❖❖❖❖❖❖❖❖❖❖❖❖❖❖❖❖❖❖❖❖❖❖❖❖❖❖

With this central clause of this fivefold formula for Eternal Life, we reach the pivot of this amazing prayer. But why call it amazing? Comforting, noble, helpful, inspiring, but not a surprising prayer. Granted that we may have been a trifle perfunctory in our use and wording of that first clause, the clause which confesses our constant awareness and reverence of Reality; granted that it does set the key and not merely describes our aim and goal but also defines our means, the means permissible if the presence of God is to be realized on earth; granted that we may not have linked the nature of the Kingdom closely enough with the nature of its King and that, in our anxiety to see our notion of right and good will done on earth, we have overlooked the governing clause, that the Kingdom on earth is to be only and all that it is in heaven; still there is nothing amazing in all this. There is only what has been called "inspired common sense," with the accent on the noun rather than on the adjective. True, we may have to do quite a great deal to ourselves before the Kingdom can come anywhere near where we are or our influence extends, and that dealing with ourselves may take a considerable time. Some of us are elderly and it takes long to teach an old dog new tricks, and the psychologists have shown us that emptying the blocked sewage system of the mind may take years. Yet the task itself, though tedious, is quite straightforward. Once we have faced up to the work of getting the skeleton out of the cupboard the worst is over. It is the first step which costs and counts and fortunately, as ours is a psychological age, we need not shrink or feel that we are being too odd or introspective. All the best people now are analyzed. It is just common sense.

And to confirm our belief that the prayer is sensible and tells us nothing that we don't know, that it puts before us only the program and the means which we have always intended to implement and employ, surely here is this third term to certify our expectations and reassure our belief. If the Kingdom must after all be allowed to have in it perhaps a certain element of "other-worldliness," if the will which is to be done is wholly God's will, and so may not be ours at all as long as we are capable of any will but His, if we shall have to do a lot more work on ourselves before we can be let work on anything more exciting and important, yet He is a kindly Father, and though we may be called upon to serve Him for a purpose and end larger and more difficult to conceive than we had assumed, He will give us adequate, comprehensible means to achieve it, and proper maintenance while we are at His work. The final goal we may not be able to appreciate or to understand, but meanwhile, as His servants He will see that we are sufficiently provided with immediate necessities. Here is this Clause Three to confirm our belief that the prayer now turns from its concern with God and His infinite purposes and our submission to them, and becomes interested in us ourselves.

But does it? Surely, what other interpretation could possibly be put upon the simple words we have always repeated from childhood? "Give us this day our daily bread." There is nothing mysterious or amazing in this request, whatever may lie in any of the four other petitions. True enough, the clause as we repeat it is the only one of the five which has a surface look of material obviousness, and that should warn us to scan it with particular care. In examining any historical document it is the main rule of the canons of historical criticism always to accept the harder reading and always to be very guarded over a passage which suddenly, after a series of profound and obscure comments, appears to fall into line with our modern outlook and our ephemeral popular notion of common sense. The same rule is present in science under the *obiter dictum*, "Beware when you find what you are looking for."

Is then this third petition as simple as it sounds and as unconcerned with the main tenor of the prayer, that absorption with God, which seems to dominate its every word? The moment we examine this clause our suspicions are confirmed. It is the strangest of all the clauses which we have till now examined. True, our current translation tries to make it sound ordinary—"daily bread," something as familiar as sunrise and as commonplace as breakfast. But there can be little doubt that the translation shows what is the fault and temptation of all translators faced with a profoundly deep saying. It makes a platitude of what is a mystery. That this phrase is a mystery there is not the slightest doubt, historically. Commentators have always been puzzled by it. On one preliminary finding they are, however, certain. The phrase is not a commonplace about common sense, a way of avoiding daily work by asking for what could and should be earned. It is asking for something of vital necessity, but something which no physical labor of ours can produce. There is an extraordinarily wide agreement of authorities on that point. From that precise and harsh doctor of the Roman Church, the Church of legal exactitude—from Jerome, the early master-textualist—down to Lutheranism's culminating modern critic Harnack, there is agreement that the term which we translate "daily bread" is a very queer Greek term. Translated exactly from the Greek it is not "daily bread" but "bread of the coming day," and Jerome and Harnack and many another student equipped with adequate textual knowledge and suspicious of mysticism have decided that this is a mysterious term—one almost untranslatable today—for it cannot apply to physical food. "The day" to which it refers is not this ordinary human morning. It is "the Day of the Lord" when the temporal night, the darkness of our human blindness, will be ended with "The Dayspring from on High." So the bread of which it speaks can only be rendered, as Jerome renders it, by some such term as the Semper-Eternal Bread. Our Lord was always speaking of that Day. His hearers were more familiar with it than pre-war Prussians were with the phrase "Der Tag." For nearly a thousand years, from before the time of the first canonical prophet Amos, the Day of the Lord had been a notion familiar to Hebrew minds. The day was to usher in the New World Order, when God would inaugurate the unending age of righteousness. This clause, then, just as much as the first two clauses, refers more to God than to man, is concerned with heaven, and only with earth as the day before heaven or the night before the Day.

But if the Bread is not farinaceous daily bread, because the Day to which it refers is beyond and above Time, what is this Bread itself? Bread is a means to life. It is the material on which life feeds. This Bread of the Coming Day can then only be the means whereby we nourish in ourselves the Life which transcends time. The Bread is the diet of those who intend to become able to live in the Kingdom. Our modern obsession with our circumstances to the exclusion of the problem of ourselves, our character, has made us forget that we may be, as we now are, unable to appreciate heaven. "The eye can only see that to which it brings the power of seeing," says Plotinus. Modern science has taught us that we can have no idea what the world is in itself. We only know how it appears to us and we already have reason to suspect that the same scene looks utterly different, to an animal, from what it looks to us. Our vision of what we call the Real, we are learning, depends far more on what we have wanted to see, wanted to find, chosen to attend to because it pleased and suited us to see things so, than on what is "objectively" there. Heaven may still be lying about us, as Wordsworth felt that it lay about him in infancy, but we have lost the power any longer to pick up that illuminating wave length. Diet also, we know, does affect and rule our physical eyes. People long kept without enough of the vitamin carried by carotin suffer from night-blindness: that ancient part of the eye which acts to guide us in the dusk goes out of action, and, what is additionally serious, we do not know that this sense has gone. The tragedy of losing a really profound sense, whether physical or spiritual, is that we do not know we have lost it, and so, treating those who still have it as frauds or fantasists, we deny ourselves the chance of recovery. When the sense of balance goes we think it is the floor which is rocking, not ourselves; when a brain tumor affects sight we think things are out of place, not that our vision is distorted and partially eclipsed.

So this clause dealing with spiritual diet is very practical—very practical and very strange. We shall see it is both of these things. Our Lord himself frequently spoke of this Bread of the Coming Day. He told his disciples that he had Bread they knew not of and he partly—but, as has been noted in the Introduction, only very initially—explained his mysterious meaning when he said, "My bread is to do the Will of Him Who sent me." When, then, we look at these phrases I think most of us, if we are frank with ourselves, feel a certain sinking. How can doing be nourishment? True, muscles grow by being exercised. But (we must repeat it, for half-truths are difficult to catch and cap and without their completing half they are as useless as is oxygen without hydrogen to slake thirst) that slogan of social service, "The best prayer is a good deed," has a serious catch in it. What can I do to wish to do a good deed? I find I have not the strength to act with real unselfishness. I find that when I act outwardly as people expect me to act I have acted from unworthy motives. I did what I did because others would disapprove if I did not. I made a choice of evils, between my dread of being disliked and my dislike of being uncomfortable. There is no good in such a shift; and yet where else shall I get the energy to behave socially except by seeing what I can get out of social approval? The wrong motive, the wish for the self's recognition, vitiates all my "unselfish" acts. It must: Can I move without my shadow moving? How am I to escape that dilemma which, as I would escape from selfishness, impales me on pride? To say that a good deed is the best prayer is all very well until we are frank enough to define exactly what a good deed is. When we see that good deeds can only be acts which are done with a complete disregard of self, then we see that the attempt to start with a good act so as to achieve the best prayer—the best prayer being of course complete, unhindered communion with God—is putting the cart before the horse. In short, to say that the best prayer is a good act is to say that the best meal for a starving man is a six-mile walk. Granted that he has been fed, then he must exercise. Having freely received he must freely give. When the body has been fed then the muscles will grow through exercise. But in an unfed body they, and the body, will simply perish if work is exacted.

Our Lord could say with complete accuracy that his Bread was to do the will of his heavenly Father. We, however, shall, I venture to think, make a tragic mistake if we equate our spiritual stature with his. One of the saddest things in the Gospel record is the indifference with which the disciples viewed the life of their Master. They have living among them this extraordinarily strange figure whose words, acts, and behavior are all quite out of the common. Yet they are not really interested in him himself. He has to extract from them their opinion as to who he is: he has to cross-question them about who he might be and what the public thought him to be. And their answers show the puzzled, listless indifference which we show when asked to explain something the importance of which seems to us not at all obvious. "Elias," "One of the prophets," "John the Baptist come to life again." Even more striking, for here, surely, the connection between the power he used for them and how he kept it must have struck them, none of them asks him how he himself prays. They know that he will often spend all night in prayer. They know that after such strange behavior he is unmistakably stranger. On one such occasion they think he is a ghost; on another that he is on fire. On a third he intervenes and saves them when some of them are in a nasty corner with a maniac they are failing to cure and only making more violent: and in this last case he actually gives them a clue which one would have thought their immediate self-concern—"Master, why could we not cast it out?"—would have made them follow up. He tells them that his transcendent power is united definitely with his power of prayer.

But they are not interested in the Man who is far more than his message. Indeed Thomas, always afraid that after all he might be trusting too much and letting his credulity lead him to dangerous lengths, wishes to short-circuit this contact with the Source of all power. He wishes to have done with these doubts and to be brought straight to the Center. "Show us the Father and it will satisfy us," he demands, wanting an end to all this vagueness. And on receiving the reply, "Have I been so long with you and have you not known me? He that has seen me has seen the Father," on receiving that astounding reply, Thomas and the rest do not seem even to have been disconcerted. "One more paradox," no doubt they reflected to themselves and turned their thoughts to practical concerns, as an animal, finding its image in the mirror has no smell, loses all interest in that strange apparition. So when the disciples became interested in prayer it was because they realized that prayer can get you things. There were tensions in that first group already showing themselves over the spoils of victory, even before they understood what the victory would cost and what it would yield. No doubt they wanted to be able to live up to the Sermon on the Mount, but they, as we, had lamentably mixed motives.

So the prayer which they were given they and we can hardly comprehend and will wrest to our own present purposes if we can. It is so against the grain of our present nature to realize that any right prayer must first and foremost be something which alters the self, a process whereby desire is transcended and the will transmuted. "Bread of the Coming Day. . . . My bread is to do the Will of Him Who sent me." How are we to do that will which is so different from ours? Are we not here involved in a vicious circle? To live as God would have us live in His eternal Life we have to do His will, but to do His will we have to become part of His Life. As long as we are self-willed, motivated by our wills, we do our wills, not His. If we are amiable and weak we try to disguise the issue and shift the responsibility by yielding to a vague uplift which says it is doing God's will, provided it is busy at some work that someone approves, provided we are serving (for whatever motive) some cause, some loyalty that we and the local majority say is for the public good. So our conscience is clear. We are not getting cash out of it, only prestige, and as for the real value to God's Kingdom of what we are doing, well, who are we to be so unpleasant as to question and set ourselves up to be better than the rest? They can carry our conscience if we give them our unsalaried services. That is a very old defense. *Vox Populi Vox Dei* was the medieval attempt to escape from the lifelong task of learning God's will and the constant risk that that will might be highly unpopular with our fellows. "Loyalty to Loyalty" is a modern philosopher's similar attempt to short-circuit that same long, steep way and bring it back to the level of heart-warming friendliness with our own people and their prejudices. If we are strong, we take over, with the defense that though this looks like ambition and tyranny it really is not, for the people's best nature is expressed in our will and we rule them only for their good. We oscillate between these two varieties of pretense: (taking whichever lie the better fits our character and, one way or the other, feeding our egos, hungry for more self-importance than self-approval can give); and that devastating realism of despairing honesty which recognizes all such activity for what it is, "pride, vain-glory and hyprocrisy" worse than the self-condemned self-indulgence of the drunkard, the sensualist, and the miser.

Hyprocrisy or despair, is there no middle way between these gulfs of destruction? There has been so much dishonesty about the reality of spiritual things, so much fraudulent issue of a paper currency backed only by a common agreement not to call the bluff, that we have to recut all these deliberately blunted, deliberately ambiguous words and print with them anew, and we have to demonstrate the value behind every promissory note. We swither between an idealism which is sham (and we know it is sham directly we come against any reality such as economic competition or war) and a realism which is despair. It is then very difficult to say anything about the mysterious word "Grace." Yet in honesty one inquirer has to own that it must be grace and nothing else about which this Clause Three is speaking. The old sacramentalists had no need to burke this question and they therefore had no doubt as to this passage's evident meaning. To Jerome, and to all who felt and feel that an outer help must come to man because his self cannot draw itself up from the trap it is in; who were also sure that such help is provided, that it does come to man when he waits without words upon God and desires only communion, an utter community with his Lord; to such traditionalists that Bread, that help, that inflowing of self-obliterating strength was the Eucharist, the supreme service of thankful union with the Eternal Life. Forms have hardened. The Eucharist of Jerome, even, was, in many details now thought important, very different from today's Mass. It trusted—as we see in his description of the vexed procedure of "reservation" for the sick—far more to a general spirit of consecrating devotion than to meticulous care as to the physical elements. The life in rigid forms too often dies. But it is clear that, through whatever channel help reaches us, it is help of what the ordinary man may well call a superhuman sort. In these words concerning the Bread something definite, if very mysterious, is being asked for, something which is not economic, something which is to bear upon the very center of the will. We may call it psychological if we remember that by that term we mean something which goes deeper than any physical need or animal hunger. For as a matter of historical fact not only does man not live by bread alone: if he attempts so to live, if he long neglects first to seek the Kingdom of God, earthly bread fails. For men turn on each other and, the constant sacrament of earth's patience and yield and man's mutual forbearance and labor being interrupted, man finds himself without even material bread. He sinks to a greater wretchedness than the "beasts that perish." Indeed, we can welcome empiricism in religion. The more we use frank inquiry into its heart, the more it is clear that we cannot do without that essence. Essential religion, communion with God and through God with all men is the only practical answer to our immediate and quite appalling problems. No other solution goes nearly deep enough.

But we must go right to the center of religion. Some three years ago there appeared an important essay on the great religions. The author took a realist approach. He judged them, not by their dogmas, but by their results, the results they could produce in the lives of their practicers. He came to an important conclusion: that those religions were effective in this respect just in so far as they employed what our parents used to call spiritual exercises. Spiritual exercises is a better term than prayer, for the word prayer has in it both the notion that as I have prayed I need do no more —a notion which ends with the praying wheel and with paying others to say my prayers—and, further, that I am free and wise to ask for what I want. That is not to say that petitionary prayer is not a very powerful instrument. Undoubtedly it is, and just for that reason it is a very advanced method and only safe in the hands of those who have attained great self-mastery in the religious life. It would seem that petitionary prayer can never be safely used by those in whom any trace of egotism still remains. As was noted in Chapter II, the chief danger lies, not in the fact that I may not be answered, but in the fact that I may, and that which answers may not be God. Spiritual exercises, on the other hand, are what everyone must employ if he would not suffocate spiritually. In a phrase, they are the deliberate methods of breathing in the Breath of Life and of exposing the individual consciousness to the radiation of the Eternal. They are the athletic and skilled exertions whereby the soul lays hold, by what is rightly called an act of devotion, and is so raised out of its self-engrossment into God's presence.

There are three stages in this treatment: first, unscreening and exposure to the Light; then, radiation, and finally, radioactivation, when that which had been radiated itself begins to be radioactive.

The author mentioned above made a second discovery which confirms many a seeker's finding. It is that such essential, working, transforming religion is like its Author, God Himself, no respecter of persons or of places. Essential religion, the actual working instructions for radiating the soul with the light of the Eternal, the actual exercises and methods and trainings whereby we expose ourselves to timeless reality, are the same whether the instructions were given in Asia three thousand years ago or in the West yesterday. The very phraseology tends to be curiously similar. The details of instruction are almost the same. Vehicles may differ, not so much from age to age as from type and stage of soul-growth.

It is this radiation, this photosynthesis of the soul, for which this clause permits us to ask. Is it possible to obtain it? Our generation is rightly skeptical of emotional conversion. We have seen too many relapses. But if we went to a radiotherapist, had one exposure, felt much better, could even show for a few days an actual erethism, the flush of the new life-giving stimulation showing on the skin, and then never went again, would we have given radiotherapy a fair trial? Could we expect any lasting benefit? Should we not expect to have a relapse, especially if we returned to that way of living which brought on the breakdown? Yet we behave in this hopelessly slipshod and feckless way in the spiritual life. We happen to be moved on some occasions; we feel better; but we do not continue and follow on with the treatment. The spiritual life is a scientific fact: it follows scientific rules. The Bread of the Coming Day must be taken day by day. Our spirits cannot stand long starvation any more than our bodies can. The Bread is a complete diet for a complete alteration of the individual being.

May we ask here, why do people who have begun fail and stop? How can we who have tasted, have felt a new power, a new hope and deliverance beginning to work in us, how do we dare lapse, how can we return to our captivity and hopelessness again? It is so common that we must try and understand the cause. "Seed sown in shallow soil"? but we are all shallow at times. How is it that some deepen and others fail to hold the sowing? Throughout these reflections on the Lord's Prayer, the standard references for insight into its meanings have been the findings of the mystic, those men and women who chose above all else to see whether, not as an abstraction of philosophy, a dogma of religion, a sanction of morality, or a hope after death, but here and now, God might be found, experienced, and known during every minute of every day. This is the one hope they cherish and the one reward they ask. But they tell us—and their accounts are ample, consistent, and mutually confirmatory—that even when the desire is as strong and single as this, the way to the tremendous goal is neither straight nor clear along its entire path. We may find whatever reasons we like to explain the fact (the mystics, who are usually empiricists, generally—sometimes too often?

—leave theorizing to the theologians) the fact remains: The way to God is a path which rises and falls; the spiritual life is one of great alternations. Even when the strictest care has been taken to avoid any faults and failings of the self, any distractions by flesh, world, or devil, when all handicaps which can be detected have been laid aside, still the progress is not constant; there are mysterious divagations, slackenings, haltings, and apparent regressions. They have been too fully described, too often and regularly noted by every mystic from the greatest to the least, for us to doubt that they are an integral part of the soul's evolution and delivery. These drynesses and darknesses must be accepted as serving a purpose in spiritual growth. That does not mean, however, that they are not very dangerous as well as distressing. It is in them that a man may lose his bearings, the very compass of his soul going "dead" in the currentless apathy in which he may find himself enfolded. But what is clear from the study of the mystics is that we should know about such states, and knowing, should be forewarned and should seek help of other voyagers to get past these stagnant and baffling spells. For they seem to be the initial cause of most of our failures—not sudden storms, for these often make us hang on more desperately to our course, but that almost imperceptible loss of momentum, that silent ebbing of vital heat, that subtle numbing, that drifting out of the full consciousness of God's being and our intention. And, we must repeat again, we are actually in a world which today is already drugged and numbed. The air is already difficult enough to breathe even if we take care to keep near the few oxygen cylinders. The cause then of most of our failures seems to be ignorance, self-assurance, and carelessness. We neglect to study the records of the dangers and risks which lie on our path; we are groundlessly sure that because we have begun with sincere enthusiasm everything will now go with increasing momentum to the goal; we overlook the first signs of oncoming failure and we delay to seek assistance. The process of becoming renewed is drastic and cannot be hurried. We have many stages to go through, all of them exacting; there is no security or any safety in resting on one's achievement until union is attained. We need expert knowledge; we have to learn much about changes in the spiritual diet as we become fitted for stronger meat. As in our physical life, so too in our spiritual, many of us struggle against weaning and want to remain infants. We have to learn how certain early helps and joys have to be discarded if we are to grow. The subject is as technical as is the obstetrician's; the process as difficult and in its way as painful as our actual birth. The knowledge and the effort have to be combined. Together they would save many losses and even more arrested growths.

Yet this process of rebirth or mutation is possible because it is natural, if not common. It is present throughout nature whenever a high social type needs to be produced and a crisis in the development of life is to be surmounted. This issue must be discussed more fully in the following chapters. Here it is enough to point out that when there is danger that the hive will be left without a queen the worker bees take an ordinary worker grub and feed it what is called the royal jelly, and the insect, which would otherwise have become only a worker bee, transmutes on the diet into a queen. The phrases "born again," "twice born," etc., have a tragic, hollow sound today. But this fundamental change in consciousness is possible and, as will be shown when we examine the next clause, is absolutely necessary, not as a private fulfillment, like learning an art, but as the one answer to chaos, the one social program that can save civilization. The chief trouble arises from the fact that we thought this mutation had to work suddenly and that after this there was nothing to be done. As a matter of fact, though sudden crises may appear, these are not essential and, what is more important, they are never final. They are generally initial symptoms. They are always signals for undertaking protracted, intelligent, clear-sighted training. They are a call, not a conclusion. So, whether the process goes by a series of shocks or by a steady pressure, the process is at basis the same. The task is nothing less than the shift of the whole being, the entire consciousness, until it alters from self-consciousness to union with the All, to God-consciousness, until the aperture of awareness, the focus of understanding, sees everything, no longer from the standpoint of the self, but from the outlook of eternity. This is a tremendous subject, not because it is vastly vague but because it is so full of detail, so crammed with particular knowledge and expert techniques. The whole of living must be and can be transformed. Has it been done? Men throughout the ages have done it and left their careful records, and men following those records are doing it, finding the records true and themselves going through this essential mutation month by month and year by year. It is a transformation not only of the will but also of the understanding; of the mind and the body as well as the soul. The last couple of generations went through something very like a dark age of spiritual knowledge. Today, however, most of us are beginning to know with some historical accuracy about a number of the major saints, and the more their records are tested the less are many of us inclined to accept the current psychologists' and psychoanalysts' explaining and explaining away of these disturbing records. As was mentioned in the introductory chapter, though many may have been overrated, a number of them, it is now clear, were supermen both in their devotion and in their powers. We cannot help being impressed. But then we turn to the good we happen to know and to the working of good in ourselves and our degree of godliness. The comparison is distinctly daunting. And self-respect, combining with caution, makes us ask, "If the saints haven't all been touched up, then were not those whose authenticity must be accepted, like poets, born, not made; and so their lives have no real reference to ours? We were not born that way and no amount of training will make us so." Dr. W. R. Inge answers that argument fairly: Reading, he says, the records of the Friends of God, we feel such a transformation of human character is hardly probable or possible. But, he adds, by what canon do we judge? By ourselves, by our way of living. We spend our lives mainly with those who can hardly be said to hunger and thirst after righteousness. Our own longing is generally more than satisfied by a couple of hours' none-too-intensive presenting of ourselves once a week. If we watch ourselves we find that we can hardly attend to anything continuously for more than fifteen seconds. So even when we present ourselves in body, our mind is most of the time absent. As we sit about in church or slump at our prayers, God is for us not nearly so real as a football match or a centipede. If we were at the one, we should be alert; if the other put a single foot on us, our attention would suddenly focus quite clearly. At least we know how the saints strove almost to the limits of safety to find their way into God's presence. Can we then rule, especially if our 1 per cent interest has brought us a gleam, that their 100 per cent devotion should not bring them fully into the Light? If I choose to live among people who never trouble to listen to music, I have the common experience that, on hearing a composition which moves a musician to tears, I am convinced it is either shallow or even disharmonious. It seldom occurs to any of us, until we are approaching mastership, to doubt whether our indifferent taste and untrained observation may not be the reason why we fail to apprehend the glory round us. A fashionable lady who knew she had as good eyes as anyone, looking at one of Turner's great attempts to paint the sunset, turned to him, remarking with polite reproof, "You know, Mr. Turner, I never see sunsets like that." His only reply is also the reply of the saints to us purblind protestors: "Don't you wish you did, Ma'am."

We have to remember and to repeat that we see that to which we attend. It is not merely our wills which are paralyzed but our understandings: our apprehension is blunted, dulled, and dimmed. This is the inevitable path of decadence and degeneracy. Cessation of function means atrophy of organ. We do not wish to explore the spiritual world. We are content sufficiently with this. And so, like wild birds left in too comfortable a habitat, we lose the wing power which would have borne us out of our bounds into the sky. One day we suddenly want our wings, but the power cannot be extemporized: spiritual sight cannot be borrowed.

Therefore this prayer, this set of rules drawn by the spirit who taught the grim parables of the Too Late—the house built on sand, the master suddenly returned at midnight, the unwise virgins—especially in this Clause Three, urges us to begin. Give us this day, this moment, and every moment, this transmuting diet. We have little time to carry out this prodigious change, and without the new birth not only our own lives but humanity itself will miscarry. When the chick has to come out of the egg there comes a time when all the food supplies are eaten. Then it must give a thousand blows and struggle out into the new life, or its home will become its tomb. Everything turns on its mysterious inner vitality—whether it is to emerge to an immensely greater life or to perish miserably. Most creatures which have to emerge from the egg die in the effort. Many are called but few can respond. Many die strangled in their own egg membranes. The tissue which should have fed them they fail to assimilate and turn into strength, and so it strangles them. This happens to many of us, with the bodily strength, the material resources, the mental endowments which we were given. What should have helped us into the new life held us, and we are trapped, in death. For one rule is absolute: you shall not stay still; up or down go you must. Each moment brings its opportunity of fuller life, but if we do not take it, if we will not move outward, then we must sink back; if we refuse to be credited with more life, we must be debited with death.

If we choose to give ourselves up to the training, we can be transformed: it is the way of life, of evolution. All that is asked of us is the wish, the absorbing wish, for the new life. We need not know precisely how it is or what it is but we must and can long for deliverance. Great endowments of physical, mental, or even moral powers, great natural aptitude to command, outstanding strength of will, of intellect, of insight, yes, even of the desire to be noble and to uplift others—all these seeming aids may actually hinder more than help. Certainly they have often deflected a life of great promise from finding God, and brought it to that self-approving futility which daily adds to atheism. What is demanded is the humility which will know itself as nothing, which will know that it itself must be liquidated that true being may be formed. The bird rising into the trackless air for the migration to its unknown home, the eel making its blind but undeflected way to its ancestral breeding ground in the Bermuda deep—open these simple brains and on their small smooth surfaces will be found no map or chart, nor in them is any compass. They go and find by following implicitly the master-urge of their nature. So it is with the soul and its end. Man is a migrant through time and satisfy him with all distractions, however much he may appear dissipated and forgetful, however many comforts and by-plays he is offered, his deepest nature stirs with anxious longing to be on its way. "But it is fantasy: there is nothing there," say the practical. "This is simply masochism," say those who attempt to staunch time with comfort. Comfort and security here!—that is the mirage. But leave the hutch, mount the air and you feel the strange but unmistakable conviction of purpose and direction suddenly irradiating you and drawing you to the unseen, inexpressible Goal. The life of doubt and vacillation then becomes the life of certitude and co-ordinated purpose, the life of accident turns into the life of meaning; chance into design; the vicious-circled self into the Infinite

Being; and time into eternity. That is the choice before us and there is no other: frustration and death or fulfillment and Life Eternal. Every activity of the soul and body must then be co-ordinated to this the true way of living. But who would live otherwise when the possibility of so living dawns on the understanding? Confronted with our tragic futility as we are, and with the immense promise of what we may be and what the Friends of God have shown us life can be, must we then not pray every day, every hour, "Give us the Bread of the Coming Day."

V. THE FORGIVENESS

"Forgive us our debts as we forgive."

✣✣✣

At this point, when we are approaching this prayer's close, need we repeat that it is very strange? In spite of nearly two thousand years of heavy use, under the worn surface-smoothness of the words, the spirit itself remains profoundly mysterious and indeed alien to our daily ways and thoughts. We have seen that its whole orientation is other than that of our common wishes and ordinary interests: it not only alters all our scale of values, taking God as the Reality and the Goal and us as the transitory appearance and the temporary means to His glory; but even the prayer's order is the reverse of our sense of order.

But when we come to this clause, surely we have found out what that order is? God first and then, when we have wholly accepted that fact, our place as channels and vehicles of His will, His light, His power. And yet if that is so, and that is certainly so, then we are faced, precisely in this clause, with a fresh difficulty and an immediate mystery. If it is essential that we should be transformed before we can be God's instruments—otherwise we must do actual harm even when we believe we are doing good—then what is this clause doing so late in the prayer, last but one of the five petitions? Surely all services, all forms of worship begin with a general confession? Yet the more we have pondered this prayer the more we have discovered that there is neither padding nor randomness about it. Not only is every clause fraught with intense meaning, but the meaning of the whole is so vital that the very order of the clauses is in itself intensely important and revealing. Each term, each petition, opens out of the one before. You cannot release each successive charge until you have discharged the one that precedes it. Indeed, the whole prayer is such a living, germinal force that we may rightly compare its structure to what today we know about that other basic germinal force, the chromosome rod which lies in the center of each life-bearing seed and which carries in it the precise potentialities of the full-grown plant or animal. We now know about the chromosomes that they carry in themselves a series of nodes or clauses—the genes —each one of which is a packet of some vital characteristic that will appear fully manifest in the developed creature which springs from the seed; and we know also that, not only is each of these genes vitally important, but the very order which they occupy in the chromosome rod is itself important and profoundly affects how they will manifest themselves in the full-grown creature.

So too it seems with this prayer: the arrangement of the clauses governs and controls the orderly and full manifestation of those powers which are necessary if we are to live according to God's will and to become what he intends we should be. First comes the acknowledgment of God's reality above all else. Right knowledge must be the foundation—a recognition of basic truth, even though we may feel that we cannot act on it or live up to it. Then there must follow the wish, the wish for God's will and rule on earth. Although we may be too helpless, too incarcerated to move, we must have a longing, a homesickness for our fatherland. Inevitably, after that there comes the longing for the power to be released from our helplessness, to be given the strength to arise and go unto our Father. Then when we act to move we discover our bonds. We find we are tied by our nature, by what we have done and been and what those have done and been who brought us up. Like a paralytic who dreams he is free, stirs in his dream, and so wakes himself to find that he is really helpless, so we will and wish and pine and strain, but our stubborn nature refuses to obey. But that effort is not vain. The strength we have been given makes us chafe at our chains. Without the spiritual food we should not have become conscious. It is the water of life and the bread of life which "bring us round." Lacking them we should continue to dream.

So the fact that forgiveness comes so late in this prayer is evidently part of its masterly design. It could not come before. Why? Because forgiveness and counterforgiveness together compose one profoundly mysterious thing. Indeed, anyone who is interested in religion is aware of that. Nothing is more noticeable than the important place which forgiveness plays in religion and the confusion which the very idea always has caused in all modern minds. In the whole of theology there is probably no doctrine which has awakened more controversy than the doctrine of the forgiveness of sin. Argumentative, individualized minds from early Buddhists to old Bernard Shaw have maintained that it must be nonsense—double nonsense —for I alone can cancel my own mistakes and no one can save me from them; nor can I or any one else save another from his mistakes. I can save myself and no one else. That argument can be made to look very sharp and clear, and doctrines of original sin, vicarious suffering, and salvation by imputed atonement can be made to look very silly, and self-contradictory. It is one of the troubles that arise from our keen limited minds and the vast indefinable experiences with which they are confronted: that the explanations which are neat and have no loose ends never cover all the facts and the explanations which accept the facts are always very un-neat and paradoxical.

Yet by far the greater part of this controversy on forgiveness arises from failure to define one's terms and to understand one's actual premises. We will think of ourselves as nothing but self-conscious individuals wholly responsible and only responsible for what each of us has done. As a matter of scientific fact that simply is not true. As a matter of practical living such a belief actually makes moral action and moral growth impossible, for it prevents me from helping anyone who may need my help below and from rising to any state above where I find myself. If I am a separate individual, a "self-made man," then, as Shaw has pointed out with perfect logic, it is a nonsensical mistake, not merely for me to seek help from my forgiveness by another, but (and this is, in fact, the converse of that proposition) for me to sacrifice myself for a lower type. I, the higher, must conserve my precious, self-won superiority, my natural endowment, and not squander it in trying, sentimentally, to help the lower, who can only drag me down. I am the superman, the higher type: the rest are waste products. But if we are, what in fact we are, members one of another, coming in to responsibilities, powers, and handicaps acquired we know not how or when; utterly dependent on others during our most formative years; throughout our lives influencing and being influenced by our fellows incessantly; in short, at the very least a hereditarily shaped, socially sustained, and group-suggestable creature—then it is absurd to act as though we were separate; then we must own that we are in constant dependence on those beyond us and in constant obligation to those behind. If we are social beings, then the analogy of the action of the free-moving, protective cells in our bodies shows how we should act and must act. When any part of the body, however distant and lowly, is invaded, the valuable white blood cells do not hold aloof and withdraw to save themselves. They crowd to the place of infection and the whole body is saved.

That example is accepted, of course, by most

socially minded people. But we must remind ourselves that it is only half the picture, one side of the complete process. Left just as it stands it, too, may become a dangerous and finally quite a misleading half-truth. Shaw and his fellow-individualists are logically right. If the picture contains nothing but the design of the white corpuscle rushing to immolate itself in defense of the attacked, wherever and whatever they are, then it is a picture which is neither true nor in the end actually inspiring. It raises two questions which truth demands shall be answered. The first is: If the higher perish for the lower, what then? Fine it may be but futile it is without a doubt. We are generally most eloquent when we are least logical. We have no right to burke hard, exact questioning. If the last word is Havelock Ellis', "Life, like all fine growths dies off at the top," the anguished question of the psalmist stands unanswered, "Wherefore hast Thou made all men for naught?" The second question rises from the first and is even more searching and practical. It brings us back to the problem already faced in the clause dealing with our diet. It asks: How do you manufacture such white corpuscles? Perhaps a few are so born and spring in a highly favorable environment, but the rest of us don't feel that way and our circumstances do not inspire us to alter our feelings. Can we be altered? How can we acquire such a capacity? As an actual fact the white corpuscles are helpless without the blood stream in which they live and move and have their being. It is the circulation of the whole body, with its secretions being poured into the blood stream, secretions, we now know, which make the white cells able to overcome infections—it is that further enlargement of the design, of the tremendous complexity and unity of a whole, which completes this picture, this analogy of the physical body and of the body politic, our whole social organism, the life of humanity, the universal Church visible and invisible.

But do we know as actually as we know that gallant men sacrifice themselves and die that there is an invisible eternal life which balances, fulfills and makes meaning of their sacrifice? A moment's consideration shows that this sentimental vagueness has arisen because we really did not wish to think too clearly about sacrifice and its meaning. Sacrifice is essential if humanity is to continue, let alone advance. The modest yield of "mutual self-interest" is never sufficient to capitalize mankind. When things are easy we can imagine that this is so but it is not so in fact: in fact we are living on the moral capital of those who sacrificed themselves in the past that we might live. And we are not even paying them the lip-reward, the ghost-money of recognizing the fact. That, then, is the actual position—they sacrificed themselves and what did they get? Fame? Thanks?

> Can storied urn, or animated bust
> Back to its mansion call the fleeted breath?
> Can Honour's voice provoke the silent dust,
> Or Flattery soothe the dull, cold ear of Death?

That is eighteenth-century reason, good sense,

and kindliness summing up about posthumous fame. It is unanswerable. "Yet men can still be made to die for it. It works." Grant that as valid; nevertheless even then the moral problem is not a whit reduced for, as we see, the vast majority, and probably the most deserving, are never memorialized, recalled, or even known. "But they did not wish to be remembered: they only wished us to be happy." It takes a good deal of impudence, of fundamental shamelessness, to say that. But it is what most of us really feel when we think about this awkward problem. We must face the proposition then. It runs: The heroes and saints died in misery and obvious immediate defeat, but it was really worth while because "they saw of the travail of their soul and were satisfied." As they sank down in agony and at an end they saw—us. Can we, dare we continue, knowing ourselves, the travesty of such a consolation? They of the prison, the torture chamber and the cross, died that we, we of the sun-beach, the racetrack, the cinema, and the restaurant, may live. It is not that we are bad or cruel or bestial. We do not need to go to any such extremes. We only need to be our healthy, futile selves to make their sacrifice a mockery, their faith —if it was only in us and the future we fulfill—a ghastly grotesque. There are some jests so bitter that they corrode worse than pain. The mouth smiles with a contortion more horrible than agony's. No, we must drop that defense. Mankind, we, are not getting better; we are not the harvest which can justify in joy their bitter sowing. If in this life, if in the gradual amelioration of manners, if in progress and "the improvement of the Spirit of the Age," these heroes and saints looked for their requital, for justification in their own lives cast away, then let us at least be truthful, if we cannot be kind or grateful or able to return their great services. If we are the meaning of the story, then it is one "told by an idiot," and they, because of their grandeur, because they would not yield and take life as it found them and drink the drugs it offers, they are of all men the most miserable, the most tragically absurd. All their sublime effort means only this, that by it they have made possible that futility at best, outrage at worst, should continue to proliferate under the pitiless sun.

These facts are indisputable. Why, then, have we refused to face them? "They are too painful. It is too cruel to expose gallant futility." True enough, if that is all the truth. But did the saints so see "the prize of their high calling"? Did they think that their reward was to be us as we are and after that the Ice Age? No, emphatically not. They said openly that they expected, rightly or wrongly, something quite other. Were they right? We are incapable of saying. We know that humanity, as it has developed, cannot be their reward; that could only be an additional purgatory. But we cannot say they were not right in what they did expect, because, to win to the station from which they took their bearings, that would be too painful for us, too painful in much more practical a sense of the word than as it is used above in reference to our fine sensibilities and our dread of exposing the futility of saintliness. The saints did not want this world unless it became heaven, unless God was always evidently present. As we saw in discussing this prayer's first clause, the mystic feels that anywhere that God is not unmistakably manifest is hell. That position is for us frankly incredible. We want this world as we see it, as it fits our daydreams, and as much of the presence of God, of Reality, as may be necessary to keep it in order and from becoming obvious bedlam. So it is natural for us to equate spiritual advance with material progress. Spirit then rapidly ceases to be something in its own right, Reality which sustains, and is not sustained by, phenomena. We like to utter such gentle vague phrases as that right action is prized at the heart of things.

But what do we mean? When Paul says harshly, "If in this life only we have hope in Christ we are of all men the most miserable," because "If Christ be not risen from the dead"—however gallant and inspiring is death—"your faith is vain; ye are yet in your sins," we say this is going too far. Do we know the first prominent churchman who said that, who brought Paul to task for talking emotional rhetoric? It was the eighteenth-century Bishop Hoadley who was then, and for years before had been, a well-fed prelate who had never entered the diocese, poor and abandoned, out of which the revenues to feed him were being extracted. Is it to be wondered at that he found such a doctrine, of the Shepherd who laid down his life for his flock and led them into Eternal Life, teaching which reeked of "enthusiasm" and superstition? Yes, the issue of the cross is actually there, in the problem, not of suffering, by itself, but of what—or what not —that suffering led to. Uncounted men were crucified; it was just a brutal form of the gallows. The cross itself, if it is the end of even the sublimest life and teaching, is nothing but failure, without the Resurrection. It is all the more bitter because of the forerunning sublimity. Wonderful, majestic, but failure. The epithets do not in fact alter the noun; it governs. Nor does the long history of the Church in any way reassure us as to the meaning of the actual tragedy of Golgotha. In brief, as all this prayer asserts, if God is not Reality, gallantry is merely goodnight. Failure in this life is failure unless there is a life more real than this, not necessarily after death but essentially outside, above, time. The cross is victory only if by it Christ finally passed by the illusion of worldly success and utopianism—men made perfect by being made comfortable in their circumstances—into eternity, and so leads the way to that state where alone lies and which alone is our salvation. It is death in order to rise in the power of endless life. It is to achieve the actual future life by breaking out of that vicious circle which is all that the best of ordinary living can yield.

We have used words so vaguely, so intentionally vaguely, that we must be harshly clear on this issue. The two points about which there must be no ambiguity, if we are to cut our way out of sham religion into true, are: (1) that we are actually members one of another and so must be saved and in turn save; (2) that being saved means being extracted out of "a body of death," out of a personality in which, if we remain, we shall perish, out of a husk from which with skilled and great help and skilled and great effort we must emerge into another condition of being, a true evolutionary advance. Once, then, we allow that we are integral parts of an immense life, a life which extends not only downward but equally upward, we have a balanced and dynamic picture, a working design. We see that we are part of a vast reciprocating process. In brief, I cannot help unless and until I am helped. I cannot forgive—it is not merely my not wanting to; it is just impossible for me to forgive—until I am forgiven. Remember even the Unjust Steward, though he failed, was started with an immense loan to help him forgive his debtor—one thousand talents against one thousand pence. What actually happens, so long as I believe I am solely myself, owing none, is that the circulation of life stops, I am cut off and I die.

It is now clear why forgiveness comes so late in this prayer. It is here, almost at the end, because it is, and must be, in one way an end process. The prayer has been getting us ready for this supreme evolutionary activity. Because we have fallen into the error of thinking of ourselves as individuals, we are completely arrested, and as long as we so think, we must stay so. The prayer faces that profound problem. Here again we see, before we can reach the problem of our paralyzed wills, we have to go deeper and uncover the fact that our understandings are actually blinded. We cannot even see the truth, much less desire it. So we are told to begin with considering actual Reality; then we come to the question, Can that Reality be manifested on earth? That brings us to the power needed to transform us so that we may be channels of God's will and not obstacles. Then at last, with the paralysis of sight and will both cleared away, with the blocked channels of our being opened, with our strangulated circulation once more linked up with the full Eternal Life, the blood and essence of Being begins to flow through us. It flows through our understanding, and the illusion of our separate egotism fades; we become conscious of being in communion with God and, reciprocally in communion with man. It flows through our wills and we can forgive; we can act as God acts, restoring freedom to the chained, life to the dead. Because we are forgiven, we can forgive: because we can forgive we are forgiven. These are not separate acts but two aspects of the one cycle of recovered Reality, recovered Being—of deliverance, not from any separate sins but from the cause of all sin—the delusory sense of the separate self undepending on God and independent of man. Blake, the mystical poet, was striving to express this mystery of actuality, this true ascent of Being when he wrote:

> And so throughout eternity
> I forgive you, you forgive me:
> As our dear Redeemer said,
> This is the Wine, this is the Bread.

We are forgiven by communion, by becoming one in the act of at-one-ment.

"But," it will be asked, "is not this a vicious circle? How can we start? We cannot operate without capital and we are bankrupt. We are engines without self-starters." We put that question because it is still hard for us to imagine that anyone saves or can save us but ourselves. Yet as an actual fact we do know that people are saved and they were not saved by themselves. Some power not themselves intervened and they were started, not on a vicious circle, but on an upward spiral, a reciprocation. Something like artificial respiration or blood transfusion did take place, and then they were free to start breathing of themselves, to begin again manufacturing their own blood. We confuse our minds with anthropomorphic notions about God and His grace. Let us follow science's law of parsimony, leave aside such speculations and focus on the actual facts. These are that power outside ourselves can and does start us once again—yes, and once and again,—as part of a vast circulating, reciprocating life and then we are free to continue voluntarily in communion, in inhaling and exhaling the Breath of Life, or we are free once more to fall into suffocation, syncope, and death.

Where did the help come from? How does it operate? Had we not better leave these questions to theologians? As Buddha said, "When you are wounded by a poisoned arrow do you ask the color or the township of the physician who is extracting it and showing you he can clean the wound?" This issue arose in the first chapter, as it must, directly prayer is realized to be something more than making good resolutions to oneself. There is a power "within" and yet at the same time "without," "Needed above all things and above all things that I know." Yes, it is a mystery, an antinomy, but it is like the other great antinomies, the frank, accurate recognition of two basic facts, each of which must be recognized, though at present our limited logic cannot demonstrably reconcile them. We should not be much surprised at this. Mystery lies at the end of every process. Our vision is, as far as pure understanding is concerned, very restricted at best. This is a spiritual world. Anyone can find out for himself, if he will try, that when he can no longer help himself there is invisible help at call, if he will turn to it and trust such assistance. He need make no assumptions which will offend his reason or even his intellectual prejudices. He need only honestly try, honestly owning that he cannot further help himself, that he is disillusioned with this self of his, finds it a treacherous sham, a "body of death," wants to be rid of it, does desire helplessly to cease to love himself and, if may be, to learn sincerely to love others.

But just accepting does not end the process; it begins it. We are starting a life where, as our spiritual vitality grows, we can assimilate more and more advanced spiritual food. We are not more self-sufficient; we are more able to leave the self and depend on God. What in practice does this mean? It means, I believe, that the process of forgiving and being forgiven does not end with the recovery of a good conscience but goes on until we are united with God. Forgiveness does not end with ending of sin, with what used to be called conversion and is now often called changing. That idea of a crisis and a completion—which led in the past to people who were obviously far from perfect calling themselves perfectionists, calling themselves people who had attained union with God—has led today to another serious mistake. When the saints call themselves sinners we tend to think that they have been a little histrionic and even momentarily insincere, carried away by the wish not to seem better than the rest of us. But it is doubtful whether anybody except a saint ever blames himself sincerely. The rest of us run ourselves down in order to be reassuringly contradicted. We know that, because we know the completely different feeling we experience when someone says about us, without a trace of insincerity, what we say about ourselves. The saints feel themselves sinners because the frost-numbed limb feels pain increase the more the blood forces its way back into the frozen veins. The more fully the divine Life pours into them, the more they experience, up to the hour of union, an agony of difference. They rejoice that God is, but, just in proportion to the vividness of this experience, they suffer that though He is, they are still other, still distant, still alien.

Hence it is that each of the three great steps—the step of purgation, when as common sinners we are forgiven our sins, our private, personally contracted debts; the step when, as a saint, we are forgiven ourselves; and the final step, when we are forgiven our whole being—the mystery of inborn evil, animal perversity and blindness, the racial tragedy, and the black problem of time itself (with this threefold issue of evil the final clause in the next chapter deals), each of these great steps is a great shedding, stripping, "naughting," a going out into darkness, a devastating conviction of failure and uselessness just when we thought we were secure and effective. Each of the three births is forerun by a death, a dark night of the soul. Hearing the saints, in the anguish of their delivery, calling out with a suffocating torment at their past righteousness which has now become, and must become, "filthy rags"—a shroud, a wrinkled, smothering skin which they must cast or die—we, new to the life of embryonic or larval goodness, think that they must be neurotic, histrionic or, perhaps, really relapsed to a base from which even we have risen. We shall be less inclined to judge those ahead of us if we realize the vastness of the ascent.

It seems clear that there are three great stages or loops in the path of deliverance through forgiveness. About the first most of us know. We are set free from obviously strangulating, morbid, mortifying states. We were dying, becoming, even our associates owned, increasingly "impossible," grotesquely self-engrossed, unremittingly resentful, a public nuisance—if we were extroverts, antisocial; if introverts, psychotic. We were restored; and in a way we are grateful. We even see that, just as we have been restored, our restoration depends on our accepting responsibility, owning we were very largely to blame, for what we tried to blame on others, and on forgiving those who we used to feel had damaged us without a cause. In fact we forgive in order that the conditional forgiveness of ourselves may become actual, valid, enduring. That state of mind is so far so good. But it is very rudimentary and, if we continue content with it, we and our society will remain arrested at a very feeble and easily over-set standard of life. Indeed, our power of forgiveness gives us an exact gauge of the level of true civilization which we have reached, a level dangerously low for human society. We have within us just sufficient of the divine good will toward men, we have permitted God to forgive us to the moderate extent that we are able, generally, just to forgive our friends when they act somewhat poorly: we can pardon them provided they apologize in reasonable time and do not, for a long while, repeat the offense. This, of course, is hardly deserving of the name forgiveness. It is simply a short-term loan with notice that it must be repaid on date or we shall foreclose on our friendship. In some cases we are not even as intentional as that. We never forgive, we simply forget, we get tired of our resentment just as we tire of being patient. This is worse than the most calculating forgiveness. For the sense of wrong and the wrong itself have never been settled. To forget and not, when the wrong is fresh and keen, cleanly and consciously to forgive, is simply to let an infected wound heal on the surface. It will break out again. It is far better never to see those we have really never forgiven than once again to go with them as friends. That is the source of endless treacheries and vendettas, of the instability and irresponsibility of our social life, of the commonness of acquaintanceship and the rarity of friendship.

That standard of forgiveness we then can see accounts for our low social standards. We have far too little of the creative forgiveness of God in ourselves to be able to pass it on with real social results, going beyond getting on with our friends; extending it to our enemies, yes, to public enemies. We must be realists: goodness is not holding its own; it is on the defensive. There is an island in San Francisco Bay. It is one of the most "written-up" islands, considering its size, in the world. It looks like a monastery. It is a monastery of evil. It is populated by men who have departed so extremely from social living and even from negative good will, who have become so actively hostile to everyone, that we dare not let them loose. What does that phenomenon mean? It means that our society can produce and does manufacture types which depart extremely from the norm. They are not insane, unhinged. No. They are resourceful, active, ready, and many of them are extremely brave. They are not passive failures. They are constantly on the watch to do what they are resolved to do—evil. We cannot cure them. Why? Simply because we do not produce their opposite numbers— men as high up, as dynamic on the side of good as they are intense, dynamic in evil. We cannot produce men who for the sake of God and for the hope of mankind will break as free as they have dared to break from social suggestion, from "the mean," from good taste and convention. We like to think that such extremes are not required of us. It would be more than a little pretentious for us to set out to be intensively, unrestrainedly good. But the idea of being mildly inoffensive, gently in good taste, keeping one's religion to oneself so that no one need ever notice one has any, is just no use. If the world were a world of little gentlemen, then it might work—though even then the achievement would be pretty dreary; such a goal would be hardly worth what it cost past pioneers to let us reach and rest.

But we face an actual world which produces at its lower end men who can claim with some right and record to be diabolic, and at its upper end— ourselves. It is painfully clear that if such a world is to balance, let alone advance, we must produce men who at the least equal these desperadoes, equal their desperation by our faith, equal and cancel their acquired diabolism by an acquired divinity. Such are the saints. They have been produced; they can be produced; and if we say that our age still produces diabolists but not saints, well then, we must and can produce the environment, the teaching, the technique, and the training which allows saints to appear—or our communities are doomed. "You can't produce genius." That objection has been met when historians considered why certain times produced great art. True, we cannot create the genius, but it evidently is often lying to hand waiting the conditions in which it may flower. The environment that attended the flowering of painting in the Renaissance in Italy and the flowering of music in Germany was the existence of a public which demanded great work, and could judge when it was given this, and could criticize even the masters when they fell below their own standards of excellence.

But what are saints? They are simply men who permit God's forgiveness to come into them so fully that not only are their sins washed out, but also their very selves, their egos, and the root of their self-will. And again, we see, the intensity of their power really to forgive is in exact proportion to the degree that they have permitted themselves to be forgiven and so brought back to God. Look for a moment at the quality of their forgiveness, what they have accepted from God and so may pass on to man. I forgive to the level that I have been forgiven, and if that level is moderate (because I made reservations in what I declared, because I only wanted to lose my vices and not myself), I can forgive only people who have offended moderately and my forgiveness helps them only moderately. If I try forgiving people who have wronged me or others intensely, I find either I can't do it at all or the quality of my forgiveness is so weak that it is either resented (as the maniac became more fierce as the disciples tried to cure him) or more often dismissed with contempt. We have not power on earth to forgive sins because we are not forgiven to that degree—to that degree that God is our sole end and our ego is no more.

Therefore we must scale the second curve of the great spiral way of forgiveness if we would ever save our social order. Only people who are still quite kindly at heart want my forgiveness, for it is still so full of self—self-complacency and self-appreciation—that it is perhaps 10 per cent the love of God and 90 per cent patronage and superiority. No wonder people don't want it, resent it. What help is it to them? How does it in any way rehabilitate them and make them capable of wishing to lose themselves, make them able to believe that there is a God Who will help them both lose and find themselves in Him? Yet, we must repeat, saints do arise, their power is in exact proportion to their power to accept God's forgiveness of their whole selves, of their social being as much as of their private acts, and such men by this their acceptance of social responsibility and guilt have power really to forgive sin. They can forgive wrongs done not only to themselves but to others just because they accept as their own the guilt of others, the wrong-doing and the wrong-suffering of the entire community. They break the vicious circle: they buy up the rotten "securities" which everyone is trying to unload on the market and thus are causing ever worse panic—and so they stop the rot.

And their forgiveness can really forgive the wrong-doer because it brings him back into the current and circulation of the Eternal Life from which he cut himself off by his wrong-doing and from which the resentment of the wronged, quite as much as his own guilt, is now driving him farther away. The saints' forgiveness has the power of reaching the banished wrong-doer and salvaging him because that forgiveness has in it two real elements which grapple him. The first element is the saints' acknowledgment of a common guilt. The more they are saints, the wider is their acceptance of common responsibility, the clearer they grasp the solidarity of mankind; everyone is their neighbor. When anyone fails, their spontaneous reaction is to point to themselves, saying in the depths of their hearts, "Lord, if thou hadst been *here* my brother had not died." The constant recognition of commonalty with every human life builds a bridge from them to the isloated wrong-doer. The second element which grasps hold of the abandoned is that the quality of their goodness is dynamic. It goes for the sinner, not in order to get a nuisance out of the way, not to save society, but to save the victimizer; not to immobilize him but permanently to mobilize his ingrown energy; not to protect a status quo but to build a city of God. The saint can show the dynamic sinner a way of life far more daring, unconventional, enterprising than any border-raid on the swag of smug and timid respectables. The saint is making an attack on the very center and citadel of the thoughtlessly secure. He aims at capturing society itself.

If, then, we are to save our social life, we must produce men so deeply forgiven that they can at least forgive, creatively discharge with a renewed will, give the conviction of new unlimited kinship and friendship to those extreme types of public enmity which our social system is producing.

That were much and would work a social revolution. Yet even that is not enough to meet our present gigantic human indebtedness, our international bankruptcy, our civilizational sinfulness. So the great spiral of forgiveness climbs still higher to its third immense range, where it passes fully into the Eternal Light. And it need do so, for we have not yet faced the supreme task of redemption, where if forgiveness fails, all the preliminary ransoming may go for nothing and be utterly undone. We have seen how the servants, "the unprofitable servants," of God forgive, in a way which keeps them fairly comfortable but does not cure evil, indeed lets the worse parts of the world (even quite close at hand) grow still worse. We have seen how the saints, the Friends of God, forgive, so that those wrong-doers who still know that they are wrong and are trying to justify themselves by saying they are trying to get their own back, faced with this real restitution, the restitution of their character, the restitution of something to believe in, to love, reverence, and serve, cannot resist that pardon, that release.

But the world today is being ruined by men who have no bad conscience, who do not feel outcasts. The outcasts are a danger to society. The danger to civilization, as it is far more embracing, is also far graver. The world, at this hour, is being driven to destruction by men of incalculable dynamic energy and will, men whose absolute control of their fellows' wills, energies, and imaginations is so hypnotic that such an ascendancy would have been unbelievable to our grandparents. So, as we have seen already with our criminal products, our world is yielding destructive types utterly unmatched by what we can produce on the constructive side. As we can find no social-worker class of equal intensity with, and so equal to salvage, our criminal class, even less can we find a leader of free men equal in appeal and singleness of aim to the dictators. Beside them and their picked apostolate, our pale good fellowship of amiable half-time interest shrinks like a pouter pigeon before a condor. So today we see that human demiurges can be produced, geniuses of will, resource, and understanding of the human heart—but only in the negative, destructive categories; in evil, not in good. Men, too, can be produced, who have all the secondary virtues of courage, temperance, discipline, prudence; indeed, who lack only the primary virtue of understanding love. In short, these men are demonic.

What is our answer? Is there any answer? To become like them? That would only mean that even if we won it would be the victory of their principles. Victory in the present war can only prove one thing—that the strongest and the most cunning side, not the most rightful, has won. What then? The answer is as it has always been, forgiveness. This is the reverse of any weak yielding. We have seen what force is needed even to salvage one criminal who knows he has public opinion against him. How much more is needed to dissolve a dictatorship? But because forgiveness is God's redemptive aspect, this work is not impossible if we choose to let Him work. We must, however, allow it to be "a pure working" as Tauler calls it. We must give Him a free hand. How? The first thing is that we must be forgiven—forgiven right through and down to the level of these men's debt. The saint, the Friend of God, saves the criminal because, and just because, the saint has been forgiven as much as the criminal has sinned; the saint has been forgiven not only his personal sins but the sins of his society for which he, as part of society, has accepted the guilt. He accepts unlimited responsibility for all the wrong done, for all the individual evil.

But there is a level above that, even. Above the Friends are the Sons. They accept, and they alone can accept unlimited liability for the whole ignorance and darkness, not simply of a particular human society, but of the whole of Life, for mistaken good as for evil, for arrested growth as for perverted development, for wrong means as well as for bad ends, for false ideals as for short-sighted greed, for failure of understanding as for weakness of will. Here is forgiveness, redemption, at its highest range, its widest span—able to reach down into hell because its trust in God goes so far that it knows if it can accept solidarity, understanding, liability with the most mistaken and the most perverse, God will accept such an acknowledgment of guilt, such a divine desire to accept the debt of all and, being given that act of faith in humanity's unity and that trust in Him, He will forgive all and unite them in the only real unity, Himself.

So we see how we climb the purgatorial mountain of forgiveness, at each level gaining power, by our being forgiven, to forgive. Does all this sound mystical and other-worldly? Mystical, yes, because mysticism means the constant recognition that Reality is not "given" but must be won, must be found; it is a rock down onto which we have to dig. But other-worldly, no. This-worldly, deadly practical, the only method which cuts to the base, all other so-called practical means being at best palliatives. In the last chapter the issue was raised, the issue of our evolution, of our necessary and actual rebirth. Here we have to face it finally and see its real necessity. We have to evolve, not merely for ourselves, not merely in order that we may individually enter on the timeless life, and so be saved from the otherwise inevitable frustration and futility as the curve of our animal life turns down into its inevitable descent. We have to evolve if human society is to last, for civilization, too, has also passed its glad, confident morning, its gay, natural expansion and unquestioning advance and its faltering, losing way, sinking. For what is our actual position as a race? We have now, for three hundred years, been producing, with ever greater speed and lack of any co-ordinating control, powers quite beyond our purpose or understanding. And so we have a civilization now whose acts are not merely bad but completely beyond its knowledge. We are continually setting going radical changes the consequences of which we are totally unable not only to prevent but even to foresee. It is clear what has happened: some fissure in consciousness, long present, has suddenly begun to widen. So a rapidly extending crevasse now yawns between understanding and power, means and ends, facts and values, meaning and resources. Our innate social sense, our inherent moral sanctions, have not only failed to keep up with our advance in physical force; they have actually shrunk, while the physical force, which they were meant to balance and control, has hypertrophied.

Is there any real answer to this basic peril? The ship is capsizing. The self-styled practical man's answer is to urge that by increasing means, enlarging powers, using more force and more violence, we shall right the ship; in other words, by *adding* to the load on the gunwale which is already touching the water the ship will be brought onto an even keel! The only sensible answer is, of course, to dress the ship, to adjust at any cost the dreadfully deranged balance. But how? We need not turn to theology or religion for the answer, the only answer. For nature itself has given it in unmistakable terms. There are only two stems of the tree of life which have risen to something like the same strange height of intense social organization as has the human stem. No other mammal or vertebrate has climbed so high. But some ants and termites have evolved into an elaborate social community. What is the essential price? Not a simple rebirth, such as the locust and many other insects go through, a skin-casting and so a renewal and enlargement. But something far more profound: a thorough, drastic, and double death and birth. The high social ant, for instance, is first hatched out as a larva, an active, healthy enough little fellow, able to enjoy itself, to eat, range at will, nip its fellows if they trespass too near its jaws and even bite its adult nurses if they are unwise enough to loiter within its reach. In short, a healthy, irresponsible, kinesthetic type, all too closely paralleled by most of our well-to-do youth. Such a type cannot sustain a social order needing "eternal vigilance" and self-abnegation. So one day it dies and the stiff and helpless form is actually buried by the adults, who themselves have gone through this process of "naughting." There it lies in its pupahood, in its cocoon, all its active structure being actually melted down, reduced, and then recast into a completely different form and nature. Then it is dug up and pulled out of its husk of cocoon, to emerge a group-devoted worker, able and alone able to sustain an intensive society. That is the only way which nature has been able to devise so that a high social life may be achieved.

The parallel between this and our civilizational crisis, and between this and the evolution of man as religion has shown it, is surely so close that we may pursue it a little further. What if we are, to start with, mere larvae? And, if we do not undergo a new birth of consciousness, a new awareness of the reality with which we are surrounded, what if we are and will remain mere grubs, only able to exploit, consume, and thoughtlessly loot social reserves which higher types made possible for us? What if the essential process of rebirth is only to be effected by a real death of the self? What if even those we dub saints and patronizingly admire while owning they cannot really change things are only transitional types, abstaining from making things worse, innocent, embryos, pupae; what if they are beings who are accepting limitations and denial because they are permitted to understand that if they will die even to premature action, yield all that they may be given a new nature, they will be raised in a new being with a new power? "For ye are dead and your life is hid with Christ in God," says Paul. Is he speaking of such an evolution and process? After all, Christianity is based on this idea which is as much the teaching of Christ as it is the teaching of Paul, that Christ himself is a firstfruit, an elder brother, an exemplar, a first emergence of a new order of beings, the "new Adam." Two things at least are certain: the one from natural history, the other from our own culminating crisis of human history. The first is that no social organization comparable to ours in complexity has ever been sustainable save by constituents who have been drastically reborn. The second is that it is now horribly clear that unless we can produce such reborn types, capable of unhesitant, effortless devotion and wisdom, our humanity is doomed. We larvae have proved, at least, our utter inadequacy.

Such is the sheer ascent, the precipitous rise to which life points us. But religion replies, Though precipitous, it can be scaled, and so only the individual finds his Eternal Life. This climb is then the mountain of the mystics. First purgation, with the deliverance from sin, but no power yet to salvage others. Then illumination, with deliverance from self and the power to let the Light stream through into the darkness of others' spirits. And finally union, with deliverance from all separation, the rising to sonship with full power on earth to forgive sins. Such we may be if we wish; such only can today redeem the world.

VI. THE END OF EVIL

"Deliver us from The Evil."

✤✤✤✤✤✤✤✤✤✤✤✤✤✤✤✤✤✤✤✤✤✤✤✤✤✤✤✤✤✤✤✤✤✤✤✤✤✤✤

Now we reach the climax of this searching prayer. It is hard for us, with our lifelong familiarity and with its millennial routine use, to see it freshly. But even under this cursory examination when we have tried to do no more, and were equipped to do no more, than to try and see it freshly, to view it as something wrought for our immediate use, charged for helping us to live the immediate Eternal Life of the Sermon on the Mount, what a complete revelation it proves to be. Within it, in epitome, there lies the whole compass and span of the spiritual life, the whole range of time from dawn to night.

We peer into these awful depths finding each clause, glazed over with familiarity, concealing an abyss of experience. If we still have any doubt that in spite of its apparent verbal commonplaceness this prayer is a revelation of the tremendous immanent reality behind the façade of common sense, this climax clause should settle the matter for good. Let us, so as to be sure we are making no unwarranted leap, once again check over our steps. We have climbed following the route this spiritual map plots for us. We started our upward ascent with the preliminary act of faith—the act of faith that there is an ultimate Reality. We take the first step in our climb when we find right knowledge. This knowledge is at first only intellectual and inductive. We come to the provisional conclusion that there is a Reality, an utter and complete Being to be found. The way does exist, though steep and narrow. It is not illusion. It leads out from a world which has shown itself to be both hideous and a phantasm, a nightmare in short. We pass then to the second step. We reach right resolve. If it is the truth that there is utter Reality then such a Reality should be manifest among us. We resolve that the will done in heaven, the state of being which is in eternity, shall come on earth. We pray with conviction, "May Thy will no longer be thwarted by me: let my name perish so Thy Kingdom come." That right resolve leads inevitably to a new and right way of life, a right regime of avowed intentional living. Every activity is now co-ordinated to that one meaning-making purpose. Thought, word, deed, and livelihood are all integrated in the single all-embracing design. The Bread of the Coming Day, the Breath of Life— these equip us with a new vitality. We become skillful athletes of the new life; we live in constant and ever wider and deeper reciprocation, being ever more deeply, more creatively forgiven of God and so being, enabled, in exact proportion, to be more deeply and creatively forgiving to our fellows.

So we find ourselves, as the prayer comes up to the final clause, stripped, equipped, and prepared to be cancelers of illusion, creatures of reality, because we ourselves have been made completely transparent transmitters of the Light. And then? Surely "then cometh the End": then comes the "Well done, good and faithful servant. . . ." The ten talents exchanged for ten cities? But no; on the contrary. Then, suddenly, when we thought we had sounded our rock and touched bottom, the whole ground gives under our feet. We were expecting that with this one more turn of the steep path up the purgatorial mountain, the sun would break through, the mountain would show itself to be indeed Pisgah, there lying at our feet would be the Promised Land and we should walk straight on and smoothly into the City of God. But no. True, the path does end off, abrupt and sheer, and the clouds open before us and at our feet we see, not comfortable Canaan, not new worlds to conquer, not pearly gates opening, but the Pit, the Abyss.

This prayer proves itself so deep and so condensed that I find I cannot at this point believe it contains any padding, vagueness, or inaccuracy. No doubt there may be mistakes of recording, errors of nomenclature, but the five great urgencies of meaning seem cut deeply and unmistakably. Therefore one must own in frankness when a passage appears to which one can attach no clear practical meaning. For myself I have found only one. It is the first part of this fifth and last clause. This petition has so strange a beginning that I wish to say honestly I cannot plumb it. Our experience with the whole prayer prevents our dismissing any phrase of it, but, if we cannot do that, then we must own that here the prayer goes clean out of our very moderate spiritual depth and stature. After all, that is not to be wondered at. Most of us are beginners in the spiritual life. Why should I be able to understand every word of a master-teacher any more than I can immediately understand every design and brush stroke of a master-painter? I view a masterpiece and note the wonderful handling, the sureness of design pervading the whole. I follow the power of composition with growing wonder and enlightenment. Then, at the climax, suddenly there is an area where the harmonies and the revelation of balanced forces appear to become involved and obscure. I do not say then, "The artist has gone beyond his powers," but "my vision is outstripped."

And this particular passage is a culmination: we are reaching toward the very heart of mystery, the height and depth of the unseen, the love of God, the fact of evil. I venture to think that in this first part of this final clause, "Lead us not into temptation," no fresh textual knowledge will help us. Indeed, one thing seems clear, when we confront the mystery of what such words can possibly mean, and that is that the mystery will be solved only by the true "Higher Criticism," that judgment and insight which comes from the higher spiritual experience and knowledge. The servant knows not what his master does. The friend is permitted insights which must be denied to subordinates. It would seem that as an actual fact few of us are good enough to know much about evil. Hence we often call things evil which, in quite a little time, prove themselves good, and often tolerate as quite harmless evils which appear as blatantly deadly to the saint. About the ultimate nature of evil we can only say, and quite unconventionally and literally, "God only knows." Does He create evil? "Does God tempt, can he?" The question has been openly asked since the early apostolic epistles and indeed long before.

I think we can say that what is being faced in this final clause is nothing less than the final supreme moral problem and indeed the problem on which turns, not only morality, but the whole meaningfulness or meaninglessness of the universe —the problem of evil. When we recognize that that is what this clause now grapples, we also realize that at our level of sub-sainthood, of servanthood, the philosophic finding must stand and cannot be overstepped: "All attempts to explain rationally the problem of evil end, not in explaining it, but in verbal attempts to explain it away." Evil as we know it will not yield its dark secret to a kind of mental chess. "We are not Saved by a smart Syllogism," said Newman. "Philosophy won't stop toothache," replies John Dewey, echoing Shakespeare. "Philosophy will bake no man's bread," said Hegel, an earlier doyen philosopher—and so set himself to sanction the Prussian state which was prepared to command stones that they become bread and to stop toothache and all illness so as to have fit conscripts. Of course natural philosophy, the real name for the activity we call science, has stopped toothache and baked bread and indeed is going, with fertilizers, close to making bread out of stone and even out of air. The real trouble lies in the fact that while it does all this it does so on the premises that the universe has no meaning, that Reality is a blind machine which for a moment you can use to grind your meal but which inevitably must in time and in turn grind you also to dust. There is a very serious confusion here in our modern thought and not so deep down that we cannot see it if we wish. What the modern philosophers are saying when they say that philosophy is not of practical use is, with unfortunate confusion of phrase, that mere strength and subtlety of thinking will not alter things or even feeling. This, of course, is contrary to natural philosophy which on one side, by thinking out new ways of doing old things, is gaining ever more fabulous power over the outer world and by another line of thought, through anaesthetics, analgesics, and "suggestion" is increasingly controlling pain. What the philosophers mean are two other things, (1) that reasoning about a thing does not alter it and (2) that, however subtly you define and closely argue, the fundamental mystery of evil and of death remains. They have not said this clearly to us but have fallen back on making inaccurate statements about the preliminary evils such as pain and hunger. For they do not want to raise the issue which lies just one step further: that of the difference between reason and vision, analysis and insight, logicians and seers.

Reason is now being used as the synonym for philosophy because some fundamental power and value is requisite and that power and value the humanist is determined shall be rationalistic, shall be demonstrable by nothing but argument from those phenomenal appearances which our ordinary animal apprehensions assume without reflection to be Reality. Reason can order experience; but it cannot add to it. If our experience is per se baffling, if we feel pain and are stricken by grief, fear disgrace and shrink from death, reason cannot alter the experience. Once insight and vision fail to breed fresh life, we try and make that useful but far too elderly, matchmaker Reason yield us new birth. Of her nature she cannot. And further, when, as we have seen, our experience in its search for the firm rock of reality finds the basic antinomies—those facts which are each of them true but which seem each to deny the other—then reason is utterly helpless. Faced with free will and predestination, time and eternity, God and evil, reason is silent. We have slipped into this lazy illegitimate way of using the word reason when we really mean right—what is morally fair and just, something which cannot be established by logic but by conscience, by intuitive knowledge. Right, to be sure, must be based not on the arguable mutual convenience that may accrue to us in so acting here and now, but on the intuitive knowledge that truth, justice, and mercy are not of the apparent world but of the basic nature of Reality. Yet in our attempt to get away from that awkward fact we go on stretching and rupturing poor reason, as appears in a common ridiculous phrase in house-letting "reasonable use of the garden vegetables." The "reason" of the landlord and that of the tenant are apt to be almost unrecognizable by their fruits.

Evil will never be explained by reason, by arguing from facts, as we, sunk in our present misapprehension, see them. The stubborn master-riddle of the deadly sphynx only yields to those who have won to a station where they may look down *sub specie aeternitatis* on the travail of time. "Why does God put me in such a desperate pass?" "Why does He permit cancer and war?" "For Him to permit, is not that for Him actually to approve?" There is nothing worse or more deadly than suppressed misgivings, misgivings which we have answered verbally but which we know we have not confronted openly. This desperate, gnawing agony of doubt goes not out to timid pretenses; indeed, it only grows more savage as we with arguments would palliate it. That diabolic despair, the despair that infests so deeply the foundations of our consciousness that our faith is itself a denial, our optimism cynicism, our gaiety the grinning masks of neurosis, goes not out unless it meets those who have spent themselves in deep prayer and night-long meditation. The saints all agree that, when they have so striven, Light has come and they have seen of the travail of the soul and been satisfied. They understood, gladly accepted, and (proof that they had faced the horror and seen to the heart of the darkest of mysteries), brought back to life a new courage, a new power of creative help, a new contagion of victory. But though they may show us by their acts that if we follow the path it is well, they may not tell us in words why and how this is so and what in logical language evil is. Indeed, it seems increasingly clear that if they did we simply would not understand the phrases. A proposition in higher mathematics which fills a mathematical mind with wonder, delight, and a deep sense of insight, repeated to the rest of us seems a meaningless jingle of sounds. We cannot see the relevance of such terms, we cannot use them, they do not fit into and furnish our minds, because our way of living has no place for such thought and its overpowering experience. Those who say (so that we can understand) cannot know. Those who do know cannot say to us until we have seen. If you had the tongue of men and angels you cannot really speak of the wonder of the sunset to a color-blind man, or of the agony of a broken spine to a child who has never tasted pain, whose every movement tells it of the joy of bodily living.

With one thought, however, we can secure that this problem shall not be prematurely closed. For we need to repeat, after all our past false complacency and our present neurosis due to dishonest repression, that a real problem which is dismissed with only a verbal solution is more dangerous than a poisoned wound which has been let heal only on the surface. One of the most accurate of modern philosophers said, "The problem of evil will be found to lie under the problem of Time." What has time to do with evil? That question shows how little we have thought about evil. Indeed, most of us think of it as being only pain and, alas, generally never trouble much about that until pain touches us. The waste and agony of life; the anthropological fact that the majority of the human race never grows up to be adult; the political fact that in the twenty-one years of "peace," since concluded in September, 1939, there were only four months when a war was not raging somewhere; the economic fact that even in the richest country in the world one-third of the population is suffering from starvation diseases, that syphilis is actually gaining: any real attempt to grasp the meaning of this statistical material we call defeatist, any real attempt to get down to the root from which such misery springs we dismiss as escapism. Oriental pessimism we call those basic summons to repentance with which the greatest of teachers begin their message: "I am here to show you sorrow and the ending of sorrow." "I come not to the whole but to the sick." The world's condition, man's estate, it is clear is far more difficult to solve and make solvent than we had thought. Evil is no surface thing of unfortunate circumstances. It is in ourselves, our natures. Freedom cannot be granted, it must be won and won every time it would be exercised. To think that we really solve it by trying to make people more comfortable is to be like a baby who thinks that by shaking the screen on which the moving picture appears he will change the picture. The screen may fall but the picture will continue to be projected till the projector is stopped. Hence the proverbial futility of revolution.

That is why the true realists, the supreme teachers who could see reality, have told us to begin at the beginning. All our work will be futile unless we first understand where we are, what are our actual premises.

We want to be realists, to face Reality, we shun being called escapists and wishful thinkers. Well then, we must have the courage to face the fact that Reality is not given us. It has to be found. "How unjust! What a trick to play on us!" As realists, however, we are debarred from escaping into complaints and self-pity. Here we are born deluded, born blind and having first to win our sight. Facing that fact led to one strange, but not senseless doctrine with which men tried to be honest about evil. There is evil which not only is not pain; there is a real ill will and malignancy in us, and further, and more mysteriously, that evil was not wholly acquired by us. It was partly inherited. That is the doctrine of original sin. We see that beside our bad acts there is also to be reckoned a bad nature. But even that does not get us to the bottom of the dark well where this grim truth dwells. Beside my acts and my nature—the perversity of human nature, its antisocial urges and treasons—there is also nature, the outer, phenomenal, temporal world. That too, if we are to be truthful naturalists, we must own is not friendly. As we see it and experience it we know it as utterly amoral. Not only do we now know that disease and malignancy did not begin with civilization or with man but go back as far as we can trace living forms[1], that complaint of body and malice of temperament seem to have infected life from its beginning, but the whole universe shows no care or design, while the designs for living as worked out in the only creatures approaching our social life—the ants and termites—indicate rather the experiments of a heartless demiurge than the guidance of a loving Father. The individual constituents are wonderfully prepared for an intense social service but their end (the nest-city) is subject to grotesque accidents and even if it escape these seems wholly futile.

Can any sense be made of all these facts which we must face? Only if we dig right down to the source and do not shrink from profound realism. Only a diagnosis which tests the projector as well as the image will lead us toward a true answer. Three evils, three ignorances, said one of the greatest of the experimental thinkers, keep man from Reality. The first is sin: the various mistaken or ill-willed acts which we commit must be stopped, and their effects mopped up before we can begin the approach. But this is only a beginning. The next evil to be tackled is the root, the immediate cause of these distracting errors—it is the

[1] See Dr. Swinton's *Symptoms of disease as shown in fossil bones.*

self itself, that will have its way. Even then, though, we have not reached Reality; we have only cleared the approach. We are looking now in the right direction but as yet cannot see. The third obstacle is not a deed or a will but wrong apprehension, illusion, blindness. We have to grow a new understanding, to learn to see actuality without the prejudice and distortion of past and future—to see it in the light of the Eternal Presence. Then and then only do we see things as they actually are and can we say truthfully and without sham sentiment: The apparent world is the real world; heaven is here; eternity is now. That is why Eckhart says, deeply and truly, the third evil is time.

Such teaching may sound too deep for us but at least it serves one immediate purpose: it does check us from the shallow dismissal of evil as a small question to be solved by better distribution or by a course of psychoanalysis, and it does guard us against the superficial dismissal of those who wrestle with this dreadful mystery as being word-spinning escapists.

Though, then, the first part of this clause passes up beyond our sense and comprehension and we must take on trust that there lies here the greatest of problems, we ourselves can just glimpse the height and depth to which we must go, when we come to where the clause re-emerges at the limit of our visibility, in its second part. This part is still very strange and very terrible, but we can see, if dimly, with what an immense thing we are confronted. Deliver us from The Evil. That is the exact translation, and again, as with the Bread of the Coming Day, the exact translators have been concerned, puzzled. Here, certainly, is a mystery as deep as that cited in Clause Three. Here, as in that clause, there is something which is too big for this world, something which passes beyond the commonplace and the everyday. This thing referred to is an immensity and at the same time there is nothing vague about it. It waits at the end of the passage; it stands across our path. Until we have settled with this watcher of the threshold, this accuser, this adversary, we cannot pass the gate. We know the constructions put upon this clause by earlier students. To nearly all men of prayer in the past this terrible phrase could only refer to some complete and culminating focus of evil, the devil. Then, as we became reassured by our comfort that there was no such thing as actual malignancy, there was no positive evil, only a lack of good, "a shadow cast by light," the clause was explained as part of the Jewish obsession about the rapidly approaching end of the world. There was to be a terrible trial, "the birthpangs of the Messiah," they sometimes called it, and then, after this awful crisis, God would interfere, the very order of nature would be changed, the wrongdoers would be judged and the righteous would enjoy eternal bliss.

Our present world crisis supports our present psychological standpoint in making this latter interpretation inadequate. We are agreed that this prayer is not the prayer of a nationalist, obsessed with the oncoming fate of his people. On the contrary, this is the prayer of one who saw deep into the heart of man and the heart of God and whose word picture, in whatever language it might be couched, was one which put time as a temporary distortion of eternity and this life and the human soul in this life as an intensely critical moment when, in spite of illusory appearances, men had to recognize the good, unmask the evil, and choose against all deceptions and temptations Eternal Life. And we today, can we, faced with the present state of a world which we thought was to progress inevitably into Utopia by an indefinite increase of its physical powers, so that moral effort would be unnecessary and personal psychological conflict and intrasocial fighting would cease—can we dismiss as "other-worldly" and ineffective the urgent order to look for the evil in the human spirit, to die to it and to be reborn before we can rebuild? The Author of this prayer, if he ever said anything that was sincere, was in deadly seriousness here. He seems assured that in spite of all our good convictions, good intentions, and preparedness there lies in wait for us something far more terrible and deceitful than we can allow; that though we say we are alert we are not attending to the side from which we are being stalked.

The crisis we are facing so complacently, the risk we are running with such light-hearted and easy-going provision, is far graver than we seem able to imagine. Time and again in his teaching he comes back to that point with intense urgency.

"Too late" is the ending of a number of his principal parables. It is not a popular conclusion for stories, to our mind. We like the notion of another chance ad infinitum, and to meet our wish we cite the infinite forgiveness of God. But we have seen that Christ's teaching of his Father's forgiveness was far from sentimental. "Unless you forgive neither will your Father, even though he is your Father, forgive." No doubt there is eternal hope, but note the epithet: it is hope in some state which transcends time. Humanly speaking (and that is as far as anyone may go who has yet to abandon his human nature and take on the divine)—humanly speaking there can be too late, there can be utter failure, irredeemable in time. So we may listen with a great sense of urgency to those repeated warnings to "work while ye have the Light: the night comes when no man may work," "Today if you will hear the voice, harden not your hearts."

The call is to awake. Something is creeping past us. Something is stealing from us. We are like men beginning to drowse in the snow. We resent being shaken, buffeted, pummeled. We want to be left alone. To be left quiet is to be left to die and, even if recovery comes, we know the agony which life exacts when it re-enters and recovers a limb which has been let become numbed by cold. This terrible Evil, then, what is it if it is not just this thing, soft and stealing as death by frost? Yet our spirit is already so numbed that that simile hardly disconcerts us. How can we, when everything looks so secure around us, wake to the urgency? Perhaps, then, it is better to repeat we are being stalked, dreaming while a pitiless force of destruction glides to where it may make its irresistible spring.

> As a lion creeping nigher
> Glares at one who nods and drowses
> By a slowly dying fire.

Perhaps an even more horrible and closer simile is better. It is hard to have the nerve to do so but if you have the detachment, watch a weasel or a stoat stalking a rabbit. Watch the beastly little tragedy right through. The rabbits are feeding, the weasel trots toward them and stops. They notice him and bolt for cover—all save one. He moves, but slowly, whimpering, panting. The weasel trots nearer. The victim begins to scream. Then with a light pounce the weasel leaps on the rabbit's back. The whole strange act is inexplicable except on the ground that the rabbit is in some way yielding to the weasel. Certainly it is not using its powers to escape. It is betrayed by something in itself. And how uncannily does its fate parallel our human disaster! Do we not all know that wretched cry of the addict, of the hypocrite, of the criminal, of ourselves, "I am trying—but look—" "I *have* tried to give it up," "I have tried to change," "I do see where I am going," "I do want to be free," "Can no one help me?" "Will no one save me?" Yes, it requires literally a superhuman effort to break out of the nightmare, to struggle out of the gas-filled room. Is not that our situation? We are drugged. It is of course ghastly to asphyxiate but there comes a time when it is *easier* to die than to struggle through and on to life. The grim empirical fact which faces us can be put in a sentence: Just by living, unless we make a constant effort, we die.

There are two forces at struggle in our double nature. The one is a force of inevitability, it tends and must lead downward. It is called scientifically the catabolic force or lapse. Almost as soon as we are born it begins to work. We start by being flexible, open, sensitive, aware; but very soon we begin to harden, close up, shut down. We find it hurts to feel too much, to sympathize too widely, to be too aware, to see too many sides of an issue. We begin to find that it is comfortable to let our minds grow back and our hearts harden. To grow after the first few years, to grow not only in nature but on into what used to be called grace, is an intense effort needing constant energy, devotion, and focus. In fact we can't do it unless we care for nothing else. We can't do it unless anything else is only permitted if it aids that co-ordinating purpose. We begin by growing of ourselves. The inherent natural urge starts us as a rocket may be started by a launching charge. But then we must carry on under our own energy and intention. Most of us don't. We pass the apex of our curve and sink. But this law and its requirement is a law of all life. The plant strives away from the pull of the earth up to the light. The fish in the river must drive against the current or go faster than it. If it floats with the current it will drown. If we do not do something with time, something by which we reach outside of time, it will do something with us and it will not be a pretty thing. We need not remind ourselves of what we have seen of easy-going people who were nice enough when young and who thought all that was necessary was just to go on trusting to life to keep one nice and young. And life left them old and nasty. There is no other alternative save the way of creative effort. Even on the most obvious showing, even leaving out death and pretending that no one really minds death itself but only being diseased and old and helpless, a nuisance—even then it is clear what intense skill, athleticism, self-control, and artistry in living we require if we are not to make a really horrible mess of living. There is no truer and grimmer judgment on life, just this life, than the stoic's motto found written in Oliver Cromwell's Bible, "He that is not getting better is getting worse." We cannot then take one moment as indifferent. We cannot refuse to play each move; if we don't play it, life plays it for us in default. Each moment is a move and if it is a mistaken one, it must be remedied at once or the remedial effort will soon amount to an agony. It is so plain, why do we delude ourselves? Because we don't want the task of thinking life out and living it out. What is the fate if we don't? The basic philosophy of most people, if you dig deep enough, is despair. Do what you will for the moment, in the end the vast blind forces "chaos and old night" must win. The rocket which is sent up must return. All life must sink to a final comprehensive entropy. Our life, as part of all life, is only a curve from childhood to second childhood. You cannot break out of the indrawing field and vortex. You cannot strike away from the wheel to which you are tied. It raised you and will sweep you down. This is untrue. The rocket need not return. But if it is to break out it must rise to critical velocity. If it can make that speed then before it is spent, it will be outside the earth's pull; it will be free. It will have become an asteroid in its own right. Then it may enter the orbit of another world if it will. If we understand what life offers us, by giving us the power of intentional growth, by leaving us still alive and energetic when the natural urges and inherent developments are over, then we need not reach the animal apex and afterward enter on the decline. We can go tangentially to the curve of animal life. We can, if we choose consciously to continue our evolution, the expansion of our consciousness, go forward, refuse to decline and enter on the Eternal Life now. And these are the only people of whom it can be said without sickly sham that they have overcome death, for they have died to the animal life and are reborn to endless life.

But though the prize is the one prize worth winning, though the penalty for missing it is to have frustrated here life's purpose for us and to be doomed to a squalid descent and decomposition, the cost, the constant cost, is so high that few pay it. This is true of all freedom, all awareness, all dexterities above the common levels of routine. A brilliant vaudeville juggler had to practice one hour a day to keep up his dexterity. He said that if by any chance he missed his practice hour one day the next day he had to double the time or take the consequences—failure in his performance and loss of his engagement. Yet we think we can achieve that full consciousness, full awareness, which is the only escape from the creeping death of the soul, if we leave our spiritual life to chance. Well, we see the results in our personal relations, in our social chaos, in our international anarchy. And remember the mental climate we are living in is rapidly deteriorating. When the thermometer is falling below zero far more care is needed to avoid frostbite than when it is only just freezing. You may then be frostbitten even before you feel painfully cold.

That, then, seems The Evil from which we stand in such desperate need of deliverance. It is the evil of time, when we say, "Oh, there is plenty of time." It is the evil of the steadily worsening times when we say, "Oh, well, times have always been bad and one must fall in with what actually happens. We've all had our boyish ideals but now we are grown-up realists." Yes, it is the evil of irresponsibility toward time when we think ourselves, "things will last our time and it will be all the same in a hundred years." The really deadly things are those things to which we have no reaction, no sense of their deadliness. So X-rays give us their deadly burn without our being even aware we are near any heat, and we cannot tell by any distant sense whether a wire is "live" and can kill us or no. Daily we must remind ourselves that all animals who have a double nature and so must be born again have to make an immense effort not to be trapped in their preliminary lower form and we must also remember that an immense number are so trapped and die. We have to do something similar (in the radical nature of the change involved and the intense protracted effort required) to the chicks and the moths and the ants that struggle out of the egg and out of the cocoon. It is, then, because this life, which we take so casually, randomly, and confusedly, is of such immense importance, because we are in actual fact standing, and will not stand much longer, at the confluence of two infinities; because the tide is running only for a little while more and then will be gone for good; it is because the risk is so great, the probability so high that we will let ourselves be lulled and drugged until it is too late and this gigantic opportunity will only dawn on us when we no longer have the power to grasp it; it is because of this supreme urgency and of the terrible difficulty of our waking up to it that we pray, "Deliver us from The Evil." Do what we will, the fumes of distraction suffocate us, the certainty of nearly everyone that life really means nothing and goes nowhere numbs us. The soft tentacles of evil wrap around us and we yield, we cease to struggle and we are sucked down to death.

There is then no middle path of decent conformity, with one's religious life as a sideline, a private idiosyncrasy. Either we are convinced that the life of God is the only life and all our efforts, actions, interests, and concerns are combined and centered on that one goal, or we are simply sinking and being dissolved in the general degenerative flux, down to the dread dead sea of the final entropy. Nothing very dramatic generally happens. That would start us into action, perhaps. No, when his Lord knew that Peter was about to sink to betray him, his master did not say, "Simon, you are going to become a monster. Simon, you will become so diabolic that you will actually deny ever having known me." No, Jesus knew the kind of degraded things an unprepared and violently frightened man will say and do, words and deeds that seem to mark him worse than a beast. But seeing into the human spirit and knowing what really takes place in the depth, Jesus understood the cause of these horrible symptoms. "Simon, Simon, Satan hath desired to have thee . . ." to make you a devil? Not at all. No, the dissolution of the soul is effected in quite another and subtler way. "Satan hath desired to have thee that he may sift thee as wheat." The wind of time will simply disintegrate you, you won't exist as a person any longer. That is the fate which overhangs every one of us. Our cleaving concentrated purpose goes to pieces. We murmur, "I expect I forgot myself," "I fear I must have given up doing that some time ago," "After all, other people don't take things so seriously, so why should I?" "After all, nearly everyone thinks life doesn't really mean anything and so as we only live once why bother to be too consistent?" That philosophy, if it may aspire to such a name, has given us already a Europe aflame, a public standard of life which already smolders with shame, disgust, and resentment, and a private life where neurosis and psychosis steadily increase. It is unmistakably clear today that there are only two choices before us: Either we make life have meaning, a single purpose, comprehensive enough to embrace our every activity and worthy of our highest achievement, or life will end us. There is no middle course any longer. But a meaning as comprehensive as that can come only from a life which has its basis beneath time. To have a picture of things, a design for living adequate to embrace and co-ordinate all our experiences, we must have a perspective so vast that the point where all the lines meet is eternity. If in this life only we have hope to make a single unifying sense of all that befalls us, we are of all men the most deluded. Nothing can really be changed in time unless the fulcrum of that change is eternity. That is why revolutions revolve ceaselessly and humanity finds itself still in the same place. You cannot row yourself across a river in a barrel. All that happens is that the harder you row the faster you spin and the river bears you ever closer to the cataract.

There is the issue unmistakably in political, in social, terms. Unless we can produce this new type our civilization, and indeed our humanity, will perish. We need not argue the issue intensively today. Of that, every day the world news convinces an increasing number of people. But very few do anything. Why? Again, because of time. Yes, the world, humanity, is collapsing but it will last my time and time is all there is. There is nothing else. Whether I make an effort or not really makes no difference. As long as there was hope in progress, or of public opinion growing in numbers and in sense to approve my fine acting, I would deny myself. But now what sense is there to it? There is none, if time is all; and that is why no effort is possible unless time is seen through. Time deludes people into the false, despairing hope that everything ends in time. It does not and cannot. It is we who, with our greed and fear, make the illusion of time. When love and understanding wholly replace greed and fear, then the illusion of time is conquered. Events then all become creative opportunities. Accident and chance disappear. But because time is an illusion which we project, we cannot be ended in time by time. That is the triumphant hope of those who accept: the terrible warning to those who decline and deny. Consciousness is *sui generis*; the human soul is timeless, eternal. It can only be resolved by rising into union with the Eternal. If it refuses to follow the destiny of its growth, to climb, then it cannot change but must repeat, trapped in the awful repetition of its willful ignorance, always maintaining that life has no meaning, no purpose, that all that befalls it is not its fault but blind accident or alien malice. It will oscillate indefinitely between trying to satisfy itself with its own deliberately delusive dream of enjoyment and striving to make its staunchless craving cease in death. What that fate must mean in terms of suffering, we who remember only such brief spells of pain and pleasure cannot imagine.

If this opportunity is missed? Life ruthlessly reduces to nothing the *forms*, the embryos which fail to emerge. But what of the irreducible consciousness? We cannot say. All we know is that the Sons of vision implore us not to wait and see. They say that all that can befall us here in dismay and despair is nothing to that state when the day of opportunity is over. An old doctrine, unpopular now. It will, however, be back again tomorrow: as a rhythmic lighthouse beam every other minute sweeps the ocean. Would we act other than we are acting if that knowledge was glaring on us at the moment? Probably not. It is the will which permits us to see. There is always light for those who want to find their course. Those who wish for dark because their life would do ill in the light will always be able to imagine that there really is no illumination. Yet for those who may be hesitating knowledge is at hand to show them how to advance. Experiment, however moderate, however tentative, shows there is a channel here. We can sound our way along it even before any high degree of illumination comes to us. But it is a choice and we must make it. We must decide which picture of things is true: the picture which shows time as being the only ultimate reality and that which shows eternity so to be. If time, as the worldling believes it to be, is illusion, then, rejecting that, we must live now as in eternity, striving to be born into its perfection, striving to find purchase on its reality. The by-product of this effort is at length a good social life. Yet even this is but a by-product and must not district us from the true aim, not the making of a more orderly environment but the creative emergence of a new creature. The creature being born must not pause halfway out of its shattered egg. The travail is severe: it is more comfortable to sit down and enjoy the first gleam of light. But if we realize that we are undergoing a new birth, a psychological deliverance, then we can realize that that birth and deliverance is into an intensity, width, and richness of being, knowing, and feeling which time and those arrested in time, caught in the eddy of its vicious circle, can never know. We need not appeal only to the saints as witnesses of this fact nor think of this state of being as something vaguely and distantly post mortem. The artist, though he may not see all its implications, knows this state. The seeker of pure truth knows it, and the saint, too, realizes it as a present immediate enjoyment. For it is not other-worldly but, with an intensity which distracted and numbed worldlings cannot know, it is this-worldly. Indeed the only people who have a right to call themselves worldly are the artists, the truth-finders, and the saints, those who give livelihood and reputation gladly if only for a moment they may see Reality. The rest of us—it is we who live in dream and fantasy, who look before and after and sigh for what is not. Even those of us who think of ourselves, because of our social importance and busyness as realists, must ask ourselves, are we too trying to escape from the intensity of actuality and the cost it requires in singleness of living by incessant, multifarious activity? This full Living Now is true eternity, eternity which is not a vast span of time or something a very long time away but the end of time now. For eternity which is the Kingdom's climate is always at hand, closer than breathing, nearer than hands or feet. It does not come to us at long last and because we have lived and died. Those things of time make no difference to it and cannot bring it nearer or make it farther by one second. Eternity is not approaching us across the days and years. It is about us, within us, and is attained the moment we turn to it, as soon as we shift focus and look through the illusion of time. The struggle to be able to turn that lock may go on for years because we cannot summon our full wills really to wish it. But man is a creator: the moment he really wishes to rise out of time eternity is here.

It is, then, to this way of living, to this Kingdom of Reality, to this will of our Father done on earth that this prayer points, and with that it leaves us confronted. If we accept the training, then this preparation permits us to be delivered from the deadly delusion in which we find ourselves to be living, then we do see that the Kingdom is already here, around us, within us, we do at last and immediately see God because we have become singlehearted. Then, no longer as a hope, a hope deferred, but in the present tense, with creative conviction, because we actually see it and live in it, we can say, and as we so say, others will be able to begin to understand how, Thine is the Kingdom and all else the pretense of pretenders; the Power, and all else is the shadow-struggle of those who dream a nightmare; and the Glory—in the timeless, unchanging Reality, the everlasting Now. Amen.

www.ingramcontent.com/pod-product-compliance
Lightning Source LLC
Chambersburg PA
CBHW050806160426
43192CB00010B/1661